D0985647

NORTHERN CITYSCAPE

With Warmest Winter Wishes,
Norman Pressman
May 3/97 Hancok, MI

In memory of my Mother

NORTHERN CITYSCAPE

LINKING DESIGN TO CLIMATE

Norman Pressman

Winter Cities Association

© 1995 Norman Pressman

All rights reserved. No part of this book may be reproduced in any form by any electronic or mechanical means (including photocopying, recording, or information storage and retrieval) without permission in writing from the author.

Printed and bound in Canada by Aljon Print-Craft Limited (Kitchener, Ontario).

Canadian Cataloguing in Publication Data

Pressman, Norman, 1939-
  Northern Cityscape

Includes bibliographical references.
ISBN 0-9698761-0-6

1. Architecture and climate.   2. City planning –
Climatic factors.   3. City planning – Canada –
Climatic factors.   4. Cold regions.   I. Winter Cities
Association. II. Title.

NA2542.P74 1995   711.4'0912'3   C94-932223-7

Cover photo by National Capital Commission (Ottawa) ©

Design by David Bartholomew

Published by
Winter Cities Association
P.O. Box 580
Yellowknife, NT – Canada X1A 2N4

CONTENTS

ACKNOWLEDGEMENTS

During the past decade, many conversations and lively debates with colleagues have contributed to my observations and thoughts on the dilemmas which confront cities during winter. Approximately ten years ago what was called the "livable winter city association" was created. Although I was its founding president, a retired Canadian journalist, John C. Royle, was the person largely responsible for its existence. He spearheaded the movement, sparked my interest in the subject, and helped me to discover that no systematic analysis of city design or planning had been undertaken in the northern hemisphere which had the aim of making urban environments truly livable. It should, therefore, be mentioned that the initiative for this book really came from John to whom I am deeply grateful. Simultaneously, the name of Dr. William C. Rogers, of Minneapolis, must be cited since he was the one who promoted the idea of "livable winter cities" on the North American continent. Ten years ago, it was due to the foresight of these two individuals that this important subject began to receive the attention it warranted for so long.

It is necessary to mention the support of the Social Sciences and Humanities Research Council of Canada which awarded me a Sabbatical Leave Fellowship during 1985 to carry out research on the theme of winter cities, as an "invited professor" at the Ecole Polytechnique Fédérale de Lausanne at its prestigious Institute for Research on the Built

Environment (IREC). Here I must thank Prof. Michel Bassand, the Institute's director. Then, again in 1987 and in 1988 this same Council subventioned travel and research which brought me into contact with many colleagues and friends throughout the circumpolar world. They all stimulated my work. Also, in 1987, the Canada Mortgage & Housing Corporation made available a grant for me to compile data on winter-induced discomfort in residential areas. This was helpful in consolidating many of my ideas. During that same year, the Dept. of Indian and Northern Affairs Canada sponsored a project on innovation for cold climates in which I was heavily involved. In 1986 I was designated as Senior Research Scholar at the University of Winnipeg's Institute of Urban Studies (made possible by Dr. Alan Artibise, who was director at the time) working on a research program for "Planning in Cold Climates".

During 1987 – a landmark year – I was most fortunate to work with my Finnish friend and colleague, Prof. Jorma Mänty of the Tampere University of Technology. Together, we edited the first comprehensive book, in English, of invited articles on the subject of "Cities Designed for Winter" – published in Helsinki in 1988. In 1991, I was invited as Senior Research Fellow to the Faculty of Architecture and Town Planning (Bouwkunde) at the Delft University of Technology where, with my Dutch colleague, Boudewijn Bach, we jointly wrote a book called "Climate-Sensitive Urban Space" – dealing with more moderate climatic zones than those found at winter latitudes, but nevertheless examining the same subject matter.

The people who have helped me in a variety of ways are far too numerous to mention. However, there are those without whose support – intellectual and, at times, financial – this work could not have reached completion. My contacts with them enabled me to speak to people – and visit projects

– who were pioneers in the "winter cities" movement. Of the many colleagues who have shared their precious time and thoughts with me, I wish to single out the following:

In Sweden – Prof. Harriet Ryd of the Royal Institute of Technology (KTH) in Stockholm, architects Pelle Hultén of Falun, Per Persson and Lars-Johan Ekelöf of Luleå, Bo Larsson (city architect of Lulea), Leif Blomquist of Stockholm, Birgit Krantz of Lund, Eva Paulsson of the architectural journal "AT", Ulla Westerberg and Mauritz Glaumann of Gävle, and Christian Hedlund of the Swedish television network in Norbotten. Also, the leading pioneer of northern design, Ralph Erskine, gave his time freely as did one of his co-architects Boris Culjat.

In Norway – Prof. Anne Brit Børve of Oslo, Peter Butenschon of Oslo, architect Ole Bernt Skarstein of Bodø, the organizers of the 1988 North Calotte Architects Symposium and of the 1990 Winter Cities Forum and ECE Colloquium held in Tromsø (especially Kai Bertheussen, Ingebjørg Hage and Petter Bakke of Tromsø, Ellen de Vibe, and Frode Sandvik), architects Eilif Bjørge and Grete Smedal of Bergen, and Arne K. Sterten, one of the Norwegian pioneers in applied climatology.

In Finland – Prof. Jorma Mänty of Tampere, Prof. Jouko Mähönen of Helsinki, Prof. Aarne Tarumaa of Oulu, Dr. Anna-Maija Ylimaula of Oulu, Seppo Heikkilä of Oulu, architect Kimmo Kuismanen of Oulu, Mikko Mansikka and Jussi Rautsi at the Ministry of Environment in Helsinki, architect Reima Pietilä of Helsinki, whose recent passing will be missed throughout the international design community, Pekka Raitanen of Helsinki and architect Bruno Erat of Espoo.

In Denmark – Jan Gehl, head of urban design at the Royal Danish Academy of Fine Arts in Copenhagen and Ole Svensson of the National Danish Building Research Institute

(SBI) in Horsholm (Housing and Urban Planning Division), Jan Birket-Smith of the Greenland Technical Organization, and architect Inngi Bisgaard of Greenland and Denmark. In Iceland – Jóhann Pálsson (parks commissioner), Sigurdur Adalsteinsson, Thorvaldur S. Thorvaldsson, Thordur Th. Thorbjarnarson, architect Geirhardur Thorsteinsson, architect Valdis Bjarnadottir, Sigurdur Gudmundsson, and architect Jóhannes S. Kjarval – all of Reykjavik.

In Switzerland – architect Gilles Barbey of Lausanne, Kaj Noschis (editor of the Swiss journal *Architecture et Comportement/Architecture and Behaviour*), Dieter Ackerknecht of the Zurich planning department, Dr. Bernard Bühler of the Basel planning department, Dr. Dietrich Garbrecht of Zurich, Plemenka Supic of the Ecole Polytechnique Fédérale-Lausanne School of Architecture, Lydia Bonanomi of IREC(Lausanne), and Dr. Roderick Lawrence of the Université de Genève.

In Canada – architect Harold Hanen of Calgary who was always a sounding board for my reflections and lectures, Prof. Annick Germain of the Université de Montréal's Institut d'urbanisme, Prof. Norbert Schoenauer of the McGill School of Architecture, Dr. Marianne Stenbaek, director of McGill's Centre for Northern Studies and Research, Michael Hough (Hough Stansbury Woodland Naylor Dance Ltd. of Toronto), Edson Andrews of Yellowknife, Michael Barton of Whitehorse, Colin Williams and Bill Waechter of Rowan Williams Davies & Irwin Inc. in Guelph, Ontario. Sincere appreciation must be extended to Mme. Annie Lüttgen of the special projects division, Mayor's Office, City of Hull, Québec for her incisive mind, enthusiasm, and useful observations which always assured a balanced perspective.

In the U.S.A. – Prof. Gary Hack of the MIT Dept. of Urban Studies & Planning (who invited me to direct a "winter design" charette), Dr. Gary Gappert of the Urban Studies Dept., the University of Akron, Weiming Lu of the St. Paul Lowertown Redevelopment Corporation in Minnesota, Bryce Klug of the architectural group ECI/Hyer in Anchorage, Allen Kemplen, consultant (Anchorage), Michael Carey, Editorial Page Editor of the Anchorage Daily News, and Prof. Madis Pihlak, landscape architect at the University of Maryland – College Park.

My final acknowledgements go to my parents – whose gifts to me were an open mind, a discerning eye, an awakened inquisitiveness and a sensitivity to the human condition – and to my wife and two children for their constant encouragement, understanding, and patience during my travels to northern destinations.

Norman Pressman
December 1994

INTRODUCTION

Natural conditions in northern countries have influenced the forms of habitation and lifestyles of their people. Harsh and cold climates, despite technological advances, have forced inhabitants to develop a sharpened awareness of nature, to practice cooperation, to conserve energy and resources, and to create urban configurations which are climate-sensitive. This is especially important in the wake of automobile-oriented growth; urban sprawl; a generally inefficient use of energy, land, and resources; and in the presence of an impoverished aesthetic.

Most architects, urban designers, and city planners, in designing projects and plans, are enmeshed in the dialectics of their own individuality – and the need to express it – and in the social dimensions of their work. This tension is an integral part of the creative process whereby time and place are fundamental points of departure. In imparting order to the city and in guiding its growth, one must always bear in mind, as well, that it is simultaneously a place for survival and spiritual sustenance, for private and collective fulfillment, and for propinquity and autonomy.

One of the major purposes of urban design and planning is to act as a mirror of cultural values and to remind us who we truly are. To raise city building to an art form, exceptional cooperation between design, project planning, and policy formulation is required. Buildings, open space, and urban context must be carefully balanced to reflect both spatial and aspatial considerations. A positive tension should be set up between form and content, project and plan, the part and the whole, the private domain and the public realm, the quality of the individual dwelling and the quality of the collective urban environment.

Mediation among these opposing elements is essential in the attempt to create "in-between" or "transitional" zones which nurture human life. These zones, in both thought and practice – lodged between abstract and concrete – constitute the broad territories of creative metamorphosis in design. They also bridge the dichotomous phenomena of solid and void, interior and exterior, static and dynamic. In order for the scale, shape, texture, and grain of a city's fabric to provide a matrix in which the simple and the monumental can co-exist harmoniously, there needs to be a clear relationship between architectural typology and urban morphology. This relationship must simultaneously incorporate functionality, consistency, aesthetic delight, identity, and vitality while remaining conscious of climatic demands.

With attention to the elements described above, this book explores what the northern city is, and ought to be. It deals with the need to produce something more humane, urbanistically speaking, than that which currently exists. It is about aspiration and inspiration, directions and strategies, intentions and results. From a theoretical perspective, its focus is upon content and form, perception and meaning, space and time, and ultimately, about what is desirable and possible. While it encompasses the necessity of linking design to climate, it is primarily about ennobling the places in which we work, live, and spend some of our leisure time.

It may be worthwhile remembering a phrase from St. Exupéry's *The Little Prince* where, referring to his rose, he says "it is useful because it is beautiful". The creation of beauty is vital for elevating the soul. Beauty, in itself, is one of the basic urban functions (in addition to managing traffic, reducing pollution, etc.). Every city should attempt to lift functional accommodation to the level of great art. As one of the prominent anthropologists of our time, Claude Levi-Strauss, has pointed out in his book *Tristes Tropiques*:

> By its form, as by the manner of its birth, the city has elements at once of biological procreation, organic evolution, and aesthetic creation. It is both natural object and a thing to be cultivated; individual and group; something lived and something dreamed; it is the human invention, par excellence.

Although they share many common elements with cities everywhere, northern cities possess characteristics which are peculiar to their locations. They should not attempt to echo stylistic trends from elsewhere but try to be themselves, expressing their regional character. They ought to impress themselves onto our senses in a positive manner, as belonging to and springing from the north, not just from anywhere.

The challenge for the next generation of city builders – and designers – will be to see to it that a mature language of urban form evolves where the grandeur and majesty of the natural conditions can be wedded to the built environment without impairing either, and always by maintaining a respect for the physical terrain, the cultural context, and the spirit of place. It will be necessary to re-establish a set of forces which can channel decisions so that the environment we produce is experienced as meaningful. The guiding principle, proposed, is to grasp the essence of place in order to understand the underlying spiritual qualities – the *genius loci* – that imbue all sites.

Teams of experts will have to tackle the problems of winter cities with the same dedication that was displayed – and can still be witnessed – by the masons of Chartres and Notre-Dame. Planning and building the meaningful northern city will take time. Discovering what needs to be done and deciding how to implement it will be part of a painful search. However, if these are our goals, there is no reason why we cannot overcome any obstacles which may impede their achievement.

Hammerfest, Norway.
A housing development, with south-facing terraces, catches each
precious ray of sunshine. At 70 degrees latitude, north of the arctic
circle, daylight is a rare commodity during winter.
Photo: N. Pressman.

Library at Stockholm University (architect, Ralph Erskine).
South-facing balcony seating areas simultaneously trap the sun and
serve as a windshield, extending the outdoor season.
Photo: N. Pressman.

A THEORETICAL BASIS FOR SETTLEMENT FORM

The urban landscape is usually dependent upon natural forces and conditions. Successful adaptation of city form to dominant natural features necessitates sensitive recognition of the limitations and constraints imposed by such features. In fact, of all the influences which impact on town form, especially under harsh conditions, the most compelling is likely to be climate. Hence, it is most sensible to base decisions, from the outset, on the natural circumstances and to utilize technology in a way that will overcome any natural hindrances.

In northern climatic regions it is essential to develop architectural structures and urban forms which are direct expressions of life's realities and demands. These must not only embody necessary and optional activities but they must also satisfy local needs which are determined by cultural views. Social values, customs, building materials, orientation, climate and site must intertwine to produce a unique weave. Amalgamation of all these components is critical to ensure that functional requirements are accommodated and lifted to the realm of artistic expression where full power of the human imagination is reached. Climate, in particular, must be given a mediating role in planning and design. It must assume a pivotal position between socio-cultural requirements and corresponding built environments.

Northern cities which must contend with lengthy winters have to seek out solutions and development strategies based on their own intrinsic values and expressions of collective existence. Hence, they should not attempt to create 'summer-like' conditions all year-round, but rather take advantage of the beauty of the winter landscape in all its various forms. Tradition should remain alive while external impulses, determined by international experience in similar conditions, should be absorbed. The resulting interventions will thus be more meaningful than those predicated on a process in which tradition is willfully abandoned. Winter cities should decisively have identities of their own, and not seek to emulate international trends in urban design, especially where these do not take into account cultural, social, or climatic factors. In harsh settings, aesthetic pleasure and spiritual sustenance are extremely important. In addition, the creation of *genius loci* – the sense of place – will be an essential ingredient if the northern city is to be characterized by its singularity and memorability, by its ability to be sustainable and ecologically sound, and by its desire to resonate with civility and full cultural richness, always evoking the spirit of time and locality.

Although many major northern cities have spawned important design philosophies and have made significant contributions to broader forms of cultural endeavor, living in the north, for many, still means dwelling on the "cultural periphery" with a set of values which may be different from those in the south or in the larger metropolis.

> Even the future will have a need for the wilderness, places of solitude and rest from a strictly digital world ... living in the north, even as an explicit choice, entails a continuous rebellion of instincts, a perpetual conflict. There is the desire to combine an anonymous urban lifestyle with the manners of the periphery. People enjoy living in towns but also wish to pick cranberries in the wilds. This conflict, along with others, enhances the work of architects in the

North. The deep-seated archetypes, the cry of the curlew, the scent of lilies-of-the-valley, rowing on a misty lake, all influence creative work (Ylimaula et al., 1993, p. 15).

To plan and design any humane city – or prepare an urban development plan – ideally requires a sound theoretical foundation which is directed by natural, social, cultural, political, economic, and technological processes. In the attempt at integrating these to create a balanced urban system in harmony with the surrounding natural forces, spatial and physical configurations will be necessary to translate the processes into tangible urban forms.

There is a paucity of such theoretical foundations upon which contemporary city planning is based. In a culture of fragmentation which is so pronounced today, the urban organism tends to be a collage of free-standing object-buildings (not often well-designed) and residual open spaces. While attempting to function in a reasonably satisfactory manner, the city scarcely conveys symbolic meaning or aesthetic delight. Furthermore, it hardly exhibits the biodiversity we crave or the nurturing qualities we desire.

At the present time, not only do we lack theories for how comfortable and sustainable cities might be built, but also we are especially in need of a suitable theoretical framework that will stimulate visions for developing healthy and rewarding climate-responsive winter cities in a variety of northern settings. Northern cities, although incorporating many widely accepted planning principles, might also have to consider applying a new winter-oriented architectural and urban grammar, giving rise to innovative ways of structuring space and activities so that energy-efficiency is increased, sociability is enhanced, and the potential to enjoy winter, in all its aspects, is fully realized.

Industrial design, architecture, urban design, and city planning should embody, evoke and transmit meaning in the

3

attempt to relate function to form, form to function, and both of these to the most authentic and deepest human needs. We should not perceive the built environment as a collection of individual objects however well designed these may be. The world around us should be conceived in a 'seamless' manner in which interior design exists in relation to buildings, buildings in relation to neighbourhoods, neighbourhoods in relation to cities, cities in relation to landscapes, with all of these combining the highest regard for human well-being.

If living conditions are to be improved in northern areas, climatic imperatives will have to be accommodated and integrated as part of the design and planning process from the outset. If town livability is sought, climatically appropriate approaches shall be required. *Bioclimatic design* – which takes into account a broad range of climate tempering resources such as site selection and planning, urban form and density, use of natural or human-modified topography, vegetation, built-up configuration, orientation, outdoor space characteristics, type and location of openings, building materials, surface colours, etc. – if properly applied, can avoid harmful or undesirable effects of climate while taking advantage of its beneficial aspects.

There are many concepts which, when properly applied, can help to produce compassionate and even exciting winter cities. These include, for example, the use of heliotropic principles whereby buildings for work and habitation should receive a maximum of precious direct sunlight, and where shadows cast by structures on other forms and open spaces should be minimized or eliminated, especially during the period of the winter solstice when daylight hours are brief. Public urban space should be exposed to sunlight and be as wind-protected as possible. Energy-conservation should be encouraged through a system of incentive measures. Snow removal should be carried out in the most

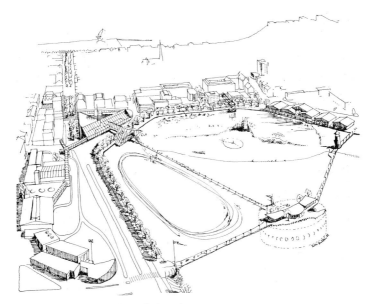

Northern Harbour of Luleå, Sweden.

Winter Development Concept Plan examines year-round uses with emphasis on the lengthy winter season.

Source: architects MAF Arkitektkontor, Luleå and Pelle Hultén.

efficient and cost-effective manner through cooperation between a city and its citizens. Ice and snow should be used in creative ways, especially for civic art, such as sculpture and urban decoration. The disposal of snow and the location of snow drifts and deposits should be carefully studied and deflected away from intensively used areas. Optimization of micro-climates should encourage greater use of outdoor public space – it is essential to extend outdoor activity during the marginal seasons (early spring and late autumn) due to the isolation caused by lengthy winters. Inside-outside relationships should be strengthened by sensitive design, creating an intermediary zone of transition which mediates between hot and cold. Pedestrian movement should occur more easily than is presently the case in most northern towns and villages. Design and dimensioning of streets, sidewalks and curbs (as well as the location of storm sewer inlets) should reflect winter, rather than summer, needs. A heightened awareness of nature, in all seasons, should be an everyday event. This can happen through outdoor educational programs such as dressing properly, winter safety knowledge, animal tracking, outdoor recreation (hiking, cross-country skiing, snowshoeing), winter sports, and a multitude of simple ways to enjoy and celebrate winter.

The intent of this book is to awaken an interest in and to promote an affection for cities in winter climates. Its primary goal is to explore the many ways in which such cities can be made attractive on a year-round basis, with special attention devoted to the winter season – which tends to receive the majority of complaints from residents and visitors alike. There is a pressing need, today, for an urban theory which enables northern cities not only to retain their inhabitants and places of employment but also to continue to appeal to those who live there, as well as to prospective dwellers attracted by job opportunities.

Not infrequently, especially in North America, cold, in urban centres, is imaged negatively while warmth is imaged positively. The text and illustrations hopefully will provide a framework that will make it possible to reverse such perceptions. In so doing, the ideas herein can form the basis for a richly textured and symbolically meaningful urban life in the northern reaches of the globe. Development policy and urban design can make significant contributions toward achieving long-term livability within a framework that is highly sustainable, possesses human scale and provides an optimum balance between *protection* from winter's hostile elements and *exposure* to its beneficial features. This is needed more than anything else at the present time, since an idealized imagery from warmer places has created a dream-like disconnection from the realities of winter life.

The following pages aim to provide deeper insights into winter-induced problems and solutions, while developing an awareness of the concepts which can improve cold-climate urban habitats − a subject still largely ignored. Through broader application of these concepts and approaches to winter city planning, further light ought to be shed on some of the future directions that northern settlement form can assume, resulting in an increasingly humanized urban landscape.

Approaches to Coping with Cold

The "indoor-living" period in some northern latitude regions has been estimated to be as high as 70% of total annual hours. Some estimates have indicated that during the long winter months, a majority of northern residents (sub-arctic regions) spend as much as 90% of their time indoors. With such extended confinement, it is particularly important to maximize positive contact with the outdoor environment.

The rhythm of urban life frequently varies with respect to climate and seasonal change. The "northern lifestyle" is seasonally variable and highly reflective of climatic reality. Socialization patterns and the use of outdoor public space in the urban north are different from their southern counterparts. Hence, plans and policies should not anticipate equal intensity for provision or use of facilities targeted toward northern users on a year-round basis.Some activities and forms of socialization even disappear during the very cold periods of mid-winter when people tend to spend more time inside the home than outside, and to engage in organized activities (work, cultural events, indoor sports, cottage-crafts, increased television watching and computer-linked activity). It has often been said that a livable home is by far the most important ingredient of a winter city. Perhaps this notion may begin to offer an explanation as to why interior design exhibits such outstandingly high quality in the Nordic countries.

Although it may not be advisable to overprotect urban dwellers from the cold, since provision of too many "artificial" environments would prove economically unfeasible and perhaps even socially undesirable, it is, nonetheless, imperative to offer a modicum of protection – and some choice – from excessive negative stressors. A healthy exposure to a variety of thermal zones within the optimal range of comfort-stress scales will result in improved states of both physiological and psychological health.

While chance conditions will always be responsible for making some winter cities more livable than others (e.g. location, micro-climatic advantages), innovative, universally applicable planning and design measures can be instituted to improve thermal comfort. The approaches adopted in one community can often be transferred to another. The common component is the adaptation of environment to extreme cold in the struggle to create living conditions which are better than merely tolerable.

Concerning adaptation to the cold, two fundamental approaches have evolved in northern latitude nations. These can be summarized as follows:

1. *Do Not Overprotect People from Nature*
This approach assumes that people must learn to co-exist with nature as satisfactorily as possible. If offered too much protection from harsh elements, humans living in cold regions will become too docile and sensitive instead of becoming adaptive, sturdy and capable of enduring nature's stresses and inconveniences without heavy reliance on technology.

2. *Offer as Much Protection as Possible*
This proposition suggests that a wide range of sheltering devices (tunnels, skywalks, arcades, gallerias, atria) should be incorporated within the existing urban fabric so that minimal contact with undesirable weather systems can be maintained. It could be inferred that humans prefer "soft", protective environments as opposed to forced contact with harsh sleet, snow, ice, wind and temperature conditions.

These represent two extreme positions. What is crucial is that *choice* be provided. There is an intrinsic beauty to winter's landscape, but not all urban dwellers are able to appreciate it (e.g. the elderly, physically-challenged, people with medical problems or allergic reactions to cold, etc.). One should have a choice of being outdoors or of withdrawing to warm, protected recesses either inside buildings themselves or in the "urban pockets" which can easily trap the sun's rays.

Architect Ralph Erskine has been one of the leading pioneers in the growing "winter cities" movement of designing with climate. In an article from the *Polar Record* for the Scott Research Institute, referring to sub-arctic urban development (Collymore, 1982, p. 26) he wrote:

> Here houses and towns should be open like flowers to the sun of spring and summer but, also like flowers, turn their backs on the shadows and the cold northern winds, offering sun-warmth and wind-protection to their terraces, gardens and streets. They should be most unlike the colonnaded buildings, the arcaded towns and matt-shadowed streets of the south Europeans and Arabs, but most similar in the basic function – helping people to maintain their skin at a comfortable 35 degrees Celsius. When studying the beautiful towns of the south, whether old or new, it is not the forms themselves which should interest us, but the inventiveness and artistry with which people solved the needs which were peculiar to their situation and time, the comfort and beauty which they created. Only by such methods can arise a personal and indigenous Alaskan, Canadian, Scandinavian or North Russian tradition.

It will be essential to explore the broadest possible range of choices available for creating a balance which protects people from and exposes them to winter's elements. In this way, human settlements can endear themselves to their inhabitants and, in so doing, appear less inhospitable.

It is most unfortunate that climate generally has been ignored in cold regions, which typically also engender highly developed economies and technological prowess (Pressman, 1987, p. 49). These two features – money and technology – have been the major means whereby inhospitable environments can be either restrained or overcome. Hardly any serious, systematic evaluation of winter-driven urban solutions has emerged until recently. In general, most developments have tended to avoid winter rather than make the best use of it, as was the case in earlier times. Today, the trend toward reducing the impact of winter in cities – or even entirely eliminating it – has virtually no technological limits. Completely enclosed city blocks and even entire neighbourhoods *can* be built. However, whether such efforts are economically feasible or socially desirable still begs discussion.

What has been referred to as "weather-sense" must clearly be an integral part of cold-culture know-how, including design. We must be capable of systematically addressing the physical, social and economic issues – translating them into built form and new urban visions – and of designating priorities and strategies for these at various scales. A new approach has to be found which not only will create a responsible northern cityscape but also will contain the seeds to propel it into the next millenium and give it the opportunity of being solidly lodged in the history of urban design.

WINTER CITIES AND CLIMATE SEVERITY

What is meant by the term "winter city"? How far north is "north"? Are there differences between what is "north" and what are considered as "northern conditions" with respect to building, planning, design and management of human settlements? There are multitudes of interpretations based on factors such as latitude, climatic elements (e.g. temperature, precipitation, wind, seasonal variation), incidence of vegetation, location of the treeline, and cultural perceptions of what constitutes "cold". For instance, Glasgow and Copenhagen, not really considered winter cities, are located at the same latitude as Moscow and Edmonton – which are among the world's coldest cities. Whitehorse and Reykjavik are at approximately the same latitude but the former is considerably colder and snowier than the latter. Toronto is situated at the same latitude as Nice and Monte Carlo but its climate, during winter, bears no resemblance to these cities on the French Riviera. Land and water mass, ocean currents such as the Gulfstream, and winds influence climate. Similarly, other elements which can be included in attempting to define "north" are the number of days of continuous permafrost, freezing periods, or permanent snow cover.

The question might be asked "what is winter"? Here again, there are no official definitions but merely interpretations. The astronomical view defines it, for the northern hemisphere, as the period from the winter solstice (December 22) to the vernal equinox (March 21). The shortest day occurs because the earth's axis is tilted as far away from the sun as it will ever be during the course of a calendar year. The climatological view accepts the division of the calendar year's twelve months into four groups of three months each – the December through March quarter known as winter. Many definitions pertain to the beginning of winter, such as the first frost or the first snowfall, with the duration of these phenomena forming the basis of a broad understanding, as vague and arbitrary as this may appear. For some, the winter is essentially seen as a season in which snow and ice-cover enable outdoor recreational and leisure activity such as skiing, skating, sledding, or even ice-fishing (Philips, 1988, p. 66).

There was a first attempt at defining "winter cities" as (Rogers and Hanson, 1980, p. 21):

> places where the average January temperature is 32 degrees F (zero Celsius) or colder.

Based on this arbitrary definition, another has sprung up which defined "winter cities" as (Winter Cities Forum, 1986, p. ii):

> places where the average January temperature is 32 degrees F. (zero Celsius) or colder, and that are generally located above 45 degrees latitude.

Generally, most winter cities tend to be located roughly at the 45th parallel and north of it (Pressman, 1985, p. 28). However, exceptions are found in communities at high altitudes, e.g. Iran, Afghanistan, Mongolia, and in mountainous regions, such as the Alpine communities of Europe, where snow and cold temperatures are found in abundance. American cities such as Denver, Colorado and other cities situated in the Northeastern States which are beneath the 45th parallel surely qualify as "winter cities", as do all Alaskan towns.

If you are in an urban settlement anywhere in the Northern half of China or Japan, the United States, the former Soviet Union, Scandinavia, Greenland, or most of Canada, you are almost certain to be in a "winter city". Winter climates vary considerably both in perception and reality. Torontonians may be impressed by the high annual snowfall levels in Ottawa or Québec City but they must contend with grayish slush for much of the winter. Oslo and Reykjavik may cringe at the intensely cold temperatures of Oulu or Edmonton while they must manage through months which have relatively little sunshine or daylight. Stockholm receives few sunshine hours during the mid-winter period but, occasionally, can be fortunate enough to experience little snow. Other cities live with ice storms, hail, freezing rain and a myriad of precipitational variations. Towns such as Bodø in north Norway experience severe wind velocities and extreme wind chill while Calgary, with its Chinook wind, can go from cold to warm temperatures in a matter of hours.

To some, winter is associated with heavy snowfall or intense, prolonged periods of cold, while to others it may be related to darkness at far northern latitudes. All of these characteristics are invariably functions of northern winters possessing both positive and negative aspects. However, a harsh, cold, winter climate is a relative notion, embodying five basic elements (ECE, 1986):

1. temperature – normally below freezing.

2. precipitation – usually in the form of snow.

3. restricted hours of sunshine and daylight.

4. prolonged periods of the first 3 elements cited above.

5. seasonal variation.

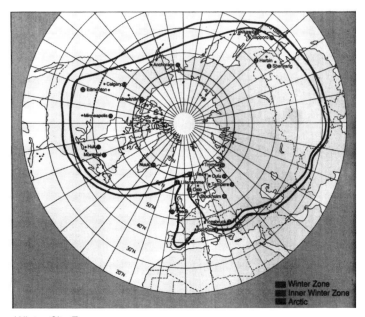

Winter City Zones.
Source: NICC Sapporo, Japan.

An acceptable definition of winter cities must assume that they are situated in regions where air temperature is below freezing, where earth is covered by snow, and where water is frozen, during a considerably lengthy part of the year. We might image the north as being generally the top quarter of the globe – the northern part of the Northern Hemisphere – inhabited by an estimated 600 million people.

The major criticism with the definition stipulating that *average* January temperature is 32 degrees F. (zero Celsius) or colder is that snow and ice may not be visible. The reason being, if night temperature falls below freezing – in which case it might snow – but day temperature is above freezing, any snow which may have accumulated during the night will have melted. Thus, there may be no continuous existence or accumulation of ice or snow and it is precisely these two elements that tend to be strongly associated with winter cities all over the globe. Therefore, based on the above, the following definition is presented (Pressman, 1988b, p. 3):

> A winter city is one in which the average maximum daytime temperature is equal to or less than 32 degrees F. (zero Celsius) for a period of at least two months or longer.

This suggests that winter normally lasts at least two or perhaps three months in length (or considerably more), and therefore incorporates the five basic elements. Furthermore, it acknowledges the fact that winter communities also exist in the southern hemisphere with "reversed seasons".

Determining Winter Severity

Knowledge about climatic variability and severity is crucial for designers and planners interested in making responsible, climate-responsive decisions. Climate – and winter – severity, if established on a comparative scale, becomes a useful concept for classification purposes. Such a notion can actually indicate relative severity for a range of locations within or between countries. The various components comprising "severity" are individually weighted and then aggregated into a single discrete value. Some of the climate stressors normally taken into account in developing a winter severity index are duration, frequency, extremes and variability with respect to hot or cold, wetness or dryness, windiness, poor air quality, continuous darkness or daylight, prolonged or intense precipitation, fog, restricted visibility, lightning and severe weather.

The Winter Severity Index can be used for a wide range of purposes, including remuneration allowances or compensation for working under severe climatic conditions, designation of localities by those suffering from weather-related illnesses, and knowledge of the data germane to planners dealing with projects related to workplaces, residences or recreational areas.

It should be stressed that one major constraint in selecting the factors representing psychophysiological parameters was the availability of data in a suitable and economically obtainable format – from already published sources or from existing machine tabulations prepared on a Canada-wide basis by the Environment Canada Atmospheric Advisory Service. In an extremely important study which attempts to design a "winter severity index", author David Philips of Environment Canada singled out four key factors considered to account for most of the direct environmental stress (Philips, 1988, p. 70):

Weighting Assigned to the Factors and Subfactors Composing the Winter Severity Index.

A. *Discomfort Factors (400 points)*
Wind Chill (170 points)
Average January wind chill based on mean wind speed and mean daily temperature

Length of Winter (115 points)
Number of months with a mean daily temperature less than 0 degrees C.

Severity of Winter (115 points)
Mean daily temperature of the coldest month

B. *Psychological Factors (100 points)*
Darkness (35 points)
Increasing darkness factor with increasing latitude

Wet Days (30 points)
Average number of days with measurable precipitation – rain and/or snow – in December, January and February

Cloudiness (10 points)
Average cloudiness (tenths) during winter: December, January and February

Sunshine (25 points)
Total hours of sunshine December, January and February (increasing sunshine factor with decreasing sunshine total)

C. *Hazardousness (100 points)*
Strong Winds (43 points)
Average wind speed of the windiest winter month

Winter Precipitation (57 points)
Total monthly precipitation when mean daily temperature is less than 0 degrees C.

D. *Outdoor Immobility (100 points)*
Fog Days (67 points)
Average number of days with fog in winter (December, January and February)

Winter Precipitation (33 points)
Total monthly precipitation when mean daily temperature is less than 0 degrees C.

Winter Severity Index for Selected Winter Cities

Anchorage	42
Beijing	22
Buffalo	48
Calgary	44
Chicago	34
Cleveland	38
Copenhagen	25
Detroit	36
Edmonton	49
Harbin	51
Helsinki	48
Indianapolis	38
Irkutsk	59
Kiev	50
St. Petersburg	50
Milwaukee	44
Minneapolis	46
Minsk	53
Montreal	49
Moscow	52
Novosibirsk	59
Oslo	42
Ottawa	50
Québec City	54
Reykjavik	38
Sapporo	41
Saskatoon	55
Stockholm	36
Toronto	43
Winnipeg	56

Winter is always a journalist's delight.

PERCEPTIONS OF WINTER

Winter tends to be perceived in many different ways – either a season to celebrate or a time to hibernate. It evokes a myriad of conflicting emotions and contradictory viewpoints (Pressman, 1992, p. 15). Poets have traditionally equated this season with the passing of life; spring with its rebirth. Within the winter season, metaphors for death are frequently found. One thing is certain, as Finnish author and poet, Toivo Pekkanen, has suggested (Pekkanen, 1962, p. 61):

> Winter is the true season of the North. Spring is only a promise that something great is about to happen; Summer is only an illusion of what people, during some hot days or weeks, at the most, believe to be true; Autumn means death, it is the dark grave of the promises of the Spring and of the illusions of the Summer. But Winter is something that really exists. It always comes back.

Cultural aspects of winter have been perceived both positively and negatively. Climate has been rumoured to significantly influence the temperament, mentality and psyche of nations. In fact, this notion was introduced on a broad scale during the latter half of the 18th century by the French philosopher Montesquieu, who claimed that the character of different nations was formed, to a large extent, by the natural surroundings and climate. This "climate doctrine" was to influence the literary scene as well as prevailing political perspectives throughout late 18th century France.

Regarding Canadian winters, French chroniclers of the 17th and 18th centuries portrayed them as unpleasant. Contemporary chansonniers and poets, song writers and authors from Québec are known for their powerful descriptions of the winters, although there is always some affection for this season displayed in their writing. The entire pattern of urban settlement and town founding, in Canada, is linked to the history of surviving winter, enduring it, and adapting to it. On the whole, it might be stated that Canadians have frequently tended to deny the existence of winter, fighting it when possible and even escaping from it – by retreating for several weeks a year to warmer climates in the southern U.S.A., the Caribbean, or the Mediterranean.

French-Canadians have been somewhat less reluctant than their English-speaking counterparts to deny the "winter fact". Well-known artists such as Cornelius Krieghoff (of Dutch origin), Robert Todd, Henry Sandham, and Clarence Gagnon, have depicted scenes of winter festivities in Québec's rural areas as well as in Québec City. Krieghoff lived in Montreal and Québec from 1845 until 1864. His paintings of the local "habitant" life embodied satirical humour with outstanding colours. His overriding themes were merrymaking, neighbours gossiping, lovers flirting on winter evenings, and Indians greeting each other on frozen rivers while Montreal gentlemen pass by on elegant sleighs (The Canadian Encyclopedia, 1985, p. 950). These paintings mirror gaiety, joie de vivre, and an almost carefree attitude exploiting the beneficial qualities of ice and snow for the sole purpose of enjoying life. The Québécois, those original colonial settlers of the frozen Canadian landscape (and whose adaptation was more 'European' of course, than that of Canada's 'First Peoples'), have accepted climate as an integral part of their cultural framework which was to evolve in a new land, far from the more temperate climate of Mother France.

*Tobogganing, Winter Scene in Montréal, c. 1885.
(artist: Henry Sandham).*
Source: National Gallery of Canada (by permission).

The Ice Cone, Montmorency Falls, c. 1850 (artist: Robert C. Todd).
Source: National Gallery of Canada (by permission).

Village in the Laurentian Mountains, c. 1924 (artist: Clarence Gagnon).
Source: National Gallery of Canada (by permission).

Winterlude/Bal de Neige, Hull, Québec.
Photo: Ville de Hull.

The most potent image perhaps ever projected of the Québécois cultural and physical landscape was by Gilles Vigneault, in his poem "Mon Pays" (My Country):

> Mon pays ce n'est pas un pays c'est l'hiver
> Mon jardin ce n'est pas un jardin c'est la plaine
> Mon chemin ce n'est pas un chemin, c'est la neige ...

> (My country is not a country, it's the winter
> My garden is not a garden, it's the plain
> My road is not a road, it's the snow ...)

Describing the harshness which winter inflicts on people, one of English-Canada's well-known poets, Alden Nowlan, wrote in the second verse of "Canadian Love Song":

> December is thirteen months long
> July's one afternoon; therefore
> lovers must outwit wool,
> learn how to puncture fur.

In 1925, A.Y. Jackson (one of the celebrated 'Group of Seven' landscape artists), in a speech entitled "Canadian Art" addressed to the Empire Club, and referring to trends of the day in painting, proudly spoke out with respect to the landscape:

> In summer it was green, raw greens all in a tangle; in autumn it flamed with red and gold; in winter it was wrapped in a blanket of dazzling snow; and in springtime it roared with running waters and surged with new life, and our artists were advised to go to Europe and paint 'smelly canals'.

Winter was frequently depicted in all its splendour by the 'Group of Seven' whether the scenes dealt with nature or with the built environment. The exquisite forms and colours of the northern regions and hinterlands are unequalled in their interpretations of seasonal variation.

In a large number of cultural contexts, the customs, ritualistic ways and social manifestations are often related to some aspect of thermal satisfaction. Certain places have traditionally been associated with activities or behaviour settings conducive to comfort-related factors, as indicated by their habitual use of space.

> The great fondness of Mediterranean cultures for their streets and plazas is largely thermal. A great deal of social life goes on in the streets and plazas because they offer the greatest thermal comfort. They provide a place to bask in the sun or a shady and airy place to be cool … . In most Mediterranean countries the custom of an evening promenade, or "paseo", developed to take full advantage of the pleasant coolness of the streets and square in the summer's evenings. (Heschong, 1985, pp. 43-44).

The sauna, reputed to have originated in Finland, was and still is essentially a place not only in which one is cleansed but also in which one may seek warmth in a very cold climate. Although the tradition of the sauna has its roots as far back as the Middle Ages, and was a place for worshipping the dead where "one must conduct oneself as one would in a church", the aspect of thermal comfort is undeniable. (Heschong, 1985, pp. 53-54). Additionally, there is the sensuous experience which accrues to the body when bathed in great doses of heat, relieving tensions and providing a place in which the family normally relaxes at least once a week. Many places possessing desirable thermal qualities tend to assume the characteristics of frequented social spaces thereby attracting people by virtue of the welcoming and hospitable climatic elements.

Northern cultures attribute many meanings to winter. In Iceland, for example, a seven month long winter, which is characterized by a lack of daylight and by constantly volatile weather systems, has certainly had a major effect on the development of a national cultural identity. Although it is not extremely cold there (the mean annual temperature in Reykjavik is 5 degrees Celsius), there is much rain – often mixed with snow – and heavy winds, especially in coastal regions. There is almost continuous daylight for a period of two to three months in summer with lengthy twilights in early spring and late fall. Normally, Icelanders consider that they have two seasons and these tend to be defined by the amount of daylight available. Winter is often associated with darkness, isolation and silence as reflected in the poetry of Vilborg Dagbjartsdottir. Harsh winters were simultaneously respected and revered, despised and feared. In many narrow fjords, the sun cannot be seen for a full two months or longer and the expectancy of awaiting the reappearing sunlight provides a unique aspect to Icelandic winters. Winter must be reckoned with. It must be acknowledged and accorded due respect if the societies exposed to it are to survive and flourish. Icelanders have constituted such a society, and it has been said that (Magnusson, 1984, pp. 240):

> From the dawn of their history winter has been one of the dominant factors in the mental as well as the physical world of the Icelanders. In every respect it has shaped their destinies, coloured their outlook and conditioned their daily existence.

In Canada, the culture has, to a significant degree, been formed by the wilderness, the immensity of the land and, often, its bareness. Much of this nation's literature and poetry is imprinted with this characteristic which can assist in a fuller understanding of the peculiarly Canadian historical character. However, this landscape is not unique to Canada alone. It seems to apply equally to Russia and parts of the former Soviet Union, and to countries such as Finland, Norway, Iceland, Sweden (and even Hokkaido, in Japan) – although much smaller by comparison.

The Finns, once having acquired independence from Russian and Swedish dominance, had to develop a cultural identity of their own, and natural landscape, lakes and forests, blue sky and white snow (colours of the national flag) were taken as self-evident symbols. The vivid ties to nature become obvious in their architectural designs which have rightfully earned world recognition through application of bold geometric forms with an extremely close relationship to and an appreciation for natural terrain features (Mänty, 1985).

Numerous aspects of everyday urban life take on negative connotations with respect to winter, since, during this season, most human activity takes place indoors – except where impractical or if there is little wind and considerable sunshine. One goes outdoors to reach the workplace or, occasionally, for recreational purposes. Snowstorms are viewed as tremendous nuisances making movement difficult if not impossible and, on the whole, they interfere with life's circadian rhythms. There has been a strong reticence to write systematically or analytically about winter, let alone to design spaces, buildings or towns to accommodate its peculiar characteristics. After all,

> People tend to take their own climate for granted. There are no records of Central Africans complaining of heat or Egyptians commenting on their extreme dryness. Western Haida Indians never once warned early European visitors to bring their raincoats (Rogers, 1986, p. 9).

Winter tends to be a season which dwellers of cold regions try vehemently to resist. The arrival of the first snow and intense cold is usually greeted with despair and a 'rejection mentality' is triggered among the population-at-large (children being an exception to the rule). Often, public behaviour reflects this disdain for winter by appearing to ignore its presence.

Contemporary society reacts negatively when the word "winter" is uttered. Dozens of jokes have evolved about this season emphasizing its less desirable qualities, and numerous quotations exist which address winter in a less than complimentary fashion (when asked to describe the seasons in Canada, a typical reply was "there are two of them – good skiing and poor skiing"). Clearly, even though winter has its aesthetic properties – clear atmosphere, snow- reflected sunlight, brilliant northern lights acting as kinetic sculpture in the skies, freshness and invigoration – it has been under constant attack, especially in urban areas, and is rarely appreciated except by a handful of nature enthusiasts who cannot wait to get into their snowshoes, ice-skates, or skis and head for the open countryside.

If we must endure, tolerate, and accept winter, then it is important to understand what needs to be done to reduce winter-induced discomfort. If we are to better respect, appreciate, and celebrate winter, we shall have to improve livability in cities during this lengthy and sometimes harsh season in a way that can help us to enjoy its beneficial qualities.

One of the various ways in which winter has been appreciated and celebrated has been through the winter carnival. Many of these carnivals – especially throughout Europe – have been rooted in pagan-based rituals dating back to the Middle Ages. Although, today, they assume a more commercial and touristic flavour, they have usually had distinct cultural derivations and meaning. Examples abound, for instance, in Switzerland, where Carnival period extends from Epiphany in early January until Ash Wednesday, the commencement of Lent – a time of fasting in Catholic regions (Swiss National Tourist Office, 1990). One famous festivity is the "Roitschäggätä" held in the Lötschental Valley of the Valais Canton in the villages of Ferden, Kippel, Wiler and Blatten on the Thursday preceding

Shrove Tuesday. Here, people wearing masks with huge pro-truding teeth and long hair, burlap sacks and furs – often carrying cowbells – do their best to frighten everyone in the surrounding villages. This is a tradition based on ancient beliefs in evil spirits living in chimneys.

Another is the Basel "Fasnacht" which starts on the Monday following Ash Wednesday with the *Morgestraich*, a strike of the clock at 4:00 a.m., when pipe-and-drum bands play in masked and costumed dress. This is said to consti-tute the largest popular festival in the country. In the spring, Zurich celebrates the "Sechseläuten", dating from the 14th century guilds. This normally occurs on the third Monday in April with members of all the ancient guilds marching, in historical costumes, throughout the city. At 6:00 p.m. sharp, they congregate at a public square near the lake and burn the "Böögg", a snowman made of wadding, symbolic of winter. Its burning marks the end of winter and the arrival of a long-awaited spring. Many of these carnivals are characterized by religious events, cold, and darkness. They conjure up winter's positive and negative aspects – highlighting and neutralizing them simultaneously.

A unique element of winter celebration has been the "ice palace". Although these have been constructed and recorded as early as the 18th century, they seemed to have reached their peak of development during the 1880s and 1890s most notably in Montreal, Québec City, and Ottawa (in Canada) and in St. Paul, Minnesota and Leadville, Colorado in the United States (Anderes and Agranoff, 1983). In a contempo-rary setting, it could be said that the City of Sapporo on the Island of Hokkaido, Japan, organized the first modern Snow Festival in 1950. It is renowned for its many full-scale, exquisite ice buildings and sculptures. Five years later, in 1955, the Québec City Winter Carnival was established with a jovial snowman – Bonhomme – symbolizing the festivity.

"Roitschäggättä" – Carnival Custom of the Lötschental/Valais.
Photo: Swiss National Tourist Office.

Sechseläuten in Zurich – the Böögg, symbol of Old Man Winter, is set on fire heralding the end of winter and arrival of spring.
Photo: Swiss National Tourist Office.

1885, Montréal Winter Carnival – Display Poster.

Photo: Notman Photographic Archives, McCord Museum of Canadian History
(by permission).

Ice Palace, Winter Carnival, Montréal, 1884.
Photo: Notman Photographic Archives, McCord Museum of Canadian History
(by permission).

Skating Carnival Composite, Montréal, 1881.

Photo: Notman Photographic Archives, McCord Museum of Canadian History
(by permission).

Place Jacques Cartier on Market Day, c. 1890, Montréal.

Photo: Notman Photographic Archives, McCord Museum of Canadian History
(by permission).

Winterlude/Bal de Neige (Ottawa-Hull).
Photo: NCC/CCN – Ottawa.

Winter Illumination in Canada's Capital.
Photo: NCC/CCN – Ottawa.

Odori Park, Sapporo during Snow Festival.
Photo: City of Sapporo.

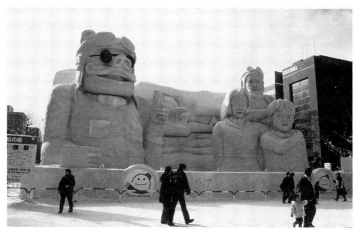

Sapporo – Japan Snow Festival.
Photo: City of Sapporo.

During the 1970s and 1980s, a host of other Canadian cities such as Sault Ste. Marie, Hull, Ottawa, Winnipeg, and St. Boniface followed suit, as did American cities in extreme winter conditions, such as Anchorage, Alaska, and Nordic towns like Tromsø, Kiruna and Oulu located respectively in the northern regions of Norway, Sweden, and Finland. The world-famous *Ididarod* race from Anchorage to Nome, in Alaska, attracts mushers, from a multitude of nations, who relentlessly drive their dog-sleds through some of the harshest wilderness imaginable. To Alaskans, this mid-winter challenge is as exciting as world-series baseball or a world-soccer cup event.

The economic impact of winter carnivals and festivals on cities and their regions can be significant. It has been estimated that the Sapporo Snow Festival generates up to US$50 million, and that visitors to the Anchorage Fur Rendez-vous spend about US$ 20 million (The Business of Winter, 1988, p. 63). The Bal de Neige/Winterlude held in the Capital Region of Hull/Ottawa has been going strong for over 10 years and nets significant tourist dollars for the regional economy. Perhaps, even more importantly, these festivals have helped to induce positive images and attitudes toward winter, especially in harsh areas where remaining indoors, for lengthy periods, is a common practice.

Native Visions of Winter

The word **Inuit** is the plural form of **Inuk** which means "man" or "person" in Inuktitut, the language spoken by the indigenous circumpolar peoples who are still sometimes (especially in Alaska) referred to as the "Eskimo" derived from Indian phraseology meaning "eaters of raw meat". It is estimated that approximately 100,000 Inuit are living in the harsh regions of the Arctic – the eastern tip of Siberia, Alaska, Greenland and Canada – about one quarter of which reside in Canada. They are usually divided into fourteen major groups with each speaking a somewhat different dialect, including **Aleuts** – from the Aleutian Islands – also an Inuit People speaking a separate language (Indian and Northern Affairs, 1975, p. 25).

Within the territories they generally inhabit, the climate ranges from an average of -25 degrees Celsius in January, reaching the freezing point between May and June, climbing to a maximum of +10 degrees Celsius in July and dipping steeply again to the freezing level in late September. Usually, the Inuit tend to think in terms of two basic seasons – summer (as brief as it may be) and winter. They are predominantly engaged in food gathering, hunting caribou and fishing. Their society was organized in such a way as to prepare food supplies available during the short arctic "warm" period prior to the onset of winter ice and darkness. With the winter imminent, they would move back to the milder coastal areas, gathering into tightly-knit groups in small villages with access to the sea which enabled seal hunting during the coldest season.

These circumpolar peoples have adjusted and adapted well to their northern environment. It has been so much a part and parcel of their normal existence that there was never a need to explicitly address its problems as has been the white man's case. One of the cornerstones of this cultural adaptation has been the kinship, friendliness, cooperation and sharing mentality of the Inuit. Winter lasts close to ten months in the Arctic. A culture which evolves from such harsh conditions understands it thoroughly. In Inuktitut there are said to be at least twenty-nine words for "ice" and approximately twenty words for "snow" (McIlroy, 1985, p. 62). The sensorial meanings ascribed to different characteristics which snow (and ice) exhibit are built into the components of the language. There are words, for instance, which express packed snow, the first snow that has recently fallen, crystalline snow, soft snow, crusty snow, sparkling snow, melting snow, snowdrifts, thawing snow, powdered snow, snow mixed with water, and so forth. Similarly, there are at least 16 terms in Norwegian which describe various types of snow – such as generic snow, wettish snow (for snowballs or snow-sculpting), snow which clings to the bottom of skis, a mix of rain and snow occurring at the freezing point, perfect snow that glitters in the sun, wind-swept snow, and so on.

The indigenous peoples inhabiting the far north embody a unique understanding of northern climatic place, the classic example being these expressions for different types of snow formations. In terms of their interpretations of the seasons – as the white man knows them – they were not based on a fixed calendar. The Inuit recognize six seasonal variations. In some regions, these carried specific names, as follows (Condon, 1983, p. 54):

1. **Ukiaktsak** – period between summer and fall.
2. **Ukiak** – fall, when the first snow arrives.
3. **Ukiok** – commencement of winter (coldest time).
4. **Opinraksak** – early spring (snow begins to melt).
5. **Opinrak** – spring (ice melts, waters are navigable).
6. **Aoyak** – summer (24 hour daylight/mild climate).

These periods of subtle climatic variation are based essentially on changing environmental parameters and are more precisely suited to a way of life determined by weather systems. During the deepest part of winter there is a maximum of socialization. With the approach of longer daylight hours and melting snow (spring), the more usual activities of hunting, fishing and working recommence. The Inuit vision of six – instead of four – seasons appears to be an effective manner for psychologically diminishing and breaking up the annual cycle. It is more finely attuned to the environmental elements and more cognizant of minor alterations occurring among the so-called seasons.

The inherited conception of Inuit life found its origin in the total dependence on nature. The sharing of the sea's catch was entirely in keeping with such a conception, as was their belief system which accepted the fact that there are certain malicious spirits and powers which constituted a danger for the living. According to these beliefs, there was life after death and Shamans, who were in touch with the invisible, had the power to drive away evil.

Not unlike the Inuit vision of an existence of six seasons, the Sami People (Lapps) – inhabiting the northern reaches of Norway, Sweden, Finland and some regions of the former Soviet Union – have traditionally recognized eight seasonal variations, analogous to those accepted by the Inuit (Manker, 1963, p. 7). The Sami seasons relate to changes in the landscape and migrations of the reindeer herds. They correspond roughly to what one might call early spring, spring, early summer, summer, late summer, autumn, late autumn and winter.

Hence, there is more than one way of regarding seasonal change or of interpreting the concept of time. Perhaps such visions of winter should play an increasingly central role within urbanized society. Options do exist in terms of the way the largely negative perceptions of the long, cold season can be manipulated. If our attitudes are to shift away from a negatively inclined posture, the manner in which we view the world around us and the language – and figures of thought – we use to identify various natural phenomena, will be critical. The ways in which we re-organize or re-structure our social systems and the physical fabric of our communities, will have to be connected to our gestalt of the northern hemisphere. Cross-cultural comparisons may be very valuable if our objective is to develop a healthier balance between technology, nature, and lifestyle.

The Northern Identity

The natural landscape – within which the built world is inserted – may exhibit intense beauty regardless of latitudinal setting. Particularly in northern regions, where seasonal variations are pronounced, every transformation provides experiential meaning and develops fresh insights for people fortunate enough to absorb such experiences. The dynamics of the natural landscape can be witnessed on at least three levels:

1. **Weather** – storms, winds, rain, snow, ice, fog, clouds, sunshine, and the nuances which these create on the landscape, including buildings and spaces enclosed by them.

2. **Seasons** – cyclical variations of the seasons reflected in dramatic climatic shifts, changing colours and forms, growth and decay, provide the annual cycle with a consistent and rhythmic unity and regular transformation.

3. **Day and Night** – shifting rhythms of brightness and darkness, morning and evening, dawn and dusk create changing moods and shapes throughout the built and natural environment.

Perhaps what is essential is to learn from nature about how to design climate-responsive spaces with a powerful relationship to people's aesthetic sensibilities. Although it is difficult to offer prescriptions to designers and planners, it is nevertheless important to realize the need to create an emotional response and attachment to place. Since we live in a universe where rational and pragmatic values, based on technological know-how and scientific methods, tend to assume greater importance than does aesthetic well-being, it is primordially crucial to emphasize "naturally-derived" solutions to the problems of winter living. Some measure of simplicity and harmony predicated on an appreciation of nature's delights must be sought as a countermeasure to decisions and interventions guided by "techno-lust". We must urgently rediscover a sense of place with climate acting as one of the primary sources of inspiration. With "facts" being stressed in our thinking and behaviour, imaginative solutions – which delight the senses – have become obligatory. After all, what could be more important than, as Christian Norberg-Schulz has articulated, to "dwell poetically?" (Norberg-Schulz, 1980, p. 202).

However, in order to understand how to dwell poetically, we shall first have to determine and even re-assess our values and priorities in terms of how we wish to relate to both the natural and built environments. We may have to re-define our identities with respect to geographical and cultural factors, embracing new visions and leitmotifs for northern places. These shall ultimately be responsible for generating the conditions essential to spiritually meaningful art – of which city building is an integral part.

It will always remain difficult to define "north" and "northern" with scientific accuracy because "actual north" defined by natural boundaries (latitudes) or physical variables (mean monthly winter and summer temperatures, vegetation regions, snowfall, etc.) will remain at variance with "psychological north" (defined by perceptual criteria such as remoteness from existing communities, the mentality of inhabitants, historical tradition and cultural attributes). The North will sometimes be viewed as a function of geographical territory and other times be seen as a derivative of either real or imagined degrees of "feeling" or "belonging".

Whatever criteria one uses to attempt definitions of "extreme" north, "far" north, or "middle" north, it is important to realize and accept that northern mentalities and lifestyles exist and that human settlements must adapt to environmentally harsh conditions if urban life is to be more than simply tolerable. Winter, indeed, is a phenomenon difficult to ignore. When leaves turn flaming red and yellow at the end of August, or even earlier, and when snow, ice, and frost are present for up to one-third of the year or longer, this most northern of seasons must be acknowledged.

In the Nordic countries, there are special ways to recognize it through events such as Lucia (mid-December) which coincides with the shortest day of the year – an artifact of the medieval calendar – a time when extra nourishment both for the body and for the soul is required. This is celebrated with ample food and drink amidst candles which burn brightly in the windows of almost every home thus illuminating the period of the long, dark nights at high, northern latitudes. Similarly, the festivity of Midsummer (June 23rd) which marks the longest day (time of the midnight sun in the far north) is warmly celebrated. It is still believed, by many, to be a night of supernatural occurrences and magical feats. But mostly, people revel in the cheer of the lengthy, bright nights gathering around the maypole where they dance to their hearts' content. The harsh, prolonged winter climate does not readily accept weakness. At the individual and societal levels there is perceived to exist a mental preparation combined with a strategic offensive for winter's onslaught which explains, to some extent, the personalities of northern peoples. It is precisely such figures of thought, engendered by winter, that are able to determine the various strains of a northern identity, and collective psyche.

CLIMATE AND ENVIRONMENT

Climate has often been called upon to explain personality, especially in extreme settings. It is believed, by many, to shape national character and even to define a common identity. Drastic shifts in weather systems affect human behaviour to more than simply a limited extent – in both hot and cold circumstances – where dramatic seasonal variations prevail. Climate has also served as a modifying or determining force in architectural and urban design. Urban form, particularly in its vernacular expression, often bears testimony to cultural and climatic influences. The essence of the vernacular approach is the application of local materials and building techniques carefully adapted to topography and climate. The result is usually a harmonious composition which strikes a balance between unity and diversity.

From the point of view of energy consumption and comfort, different climates require varying building and urban forms. In hot climates, shaded and cool, airy spaces – such as verandas, arcaded streets, and courtyards – are desirable. Much traditional warm-region architecture exhibits such design gestures. The labyrinth-like urban form, shared by virtually all cities in the Islamic world, is an excellent example. With its narrow streets providing access to private courtyard dwellings – protected from the hot sunshine – it is the dialectic opposite of the Western rationality and efficiency of the gridiron plan's organization. Invariably more intriguing and interesting than the checkerboard pattern, it is decidedly more climate-sensitive, with its "introverted" form. Its spatial pattern derives largely from climatic dictates, common religious precepts, a rigorous legal code, and consequent lifestyles. Traditional materials and natural cooling arrangements promote indigenous forms such as ventilated roofs and high thermal capacity mud-brick buildings – farther south in the Sahara. The higher the form of expression between people and their natural environments, the more significant the cultural landscape becomes.

It is well known that the effects of climatic changes upon human behaviour are considerable, both under extremes of heat and cold, as well as humidity. Northern latitude communities, such as Reykjavik, Tromsø, or Yellowknife, suffer from a lack of daylight especially during the period of midwinter. These dark, gloomy months induce a melancholy which Stockholmers call Lapp-sickness. Mental health problems increase, particularly depression – accompanied by alcoholism, drunkenness, violence and suicide. Brightness or light intensity is known to have major effects on human response – with intense light evoking increased activity; and low brightness being associated with relaxation, fatigue and sleep.

Special winds can have an impact on behavioural responses – usually of a negative nature – of regional populations subjected to them. One such wind is the frequently cited "foehn" (hot winds supposedly originating in the Sahara, blowing from the south of Europe across Italy and down the northern valleys of the Alpine ranges). The "foehn" is a complex phenomenon acting on the human organism at various levels. Its influence is clearly measurable through the physical reactions it induces with psychological effects also present. People are known to have reported discomfort, short tempers, and a range of weather-related complaints as a result of this wind.

Human mobility is affected by weather especially where it has a tendency to be adverse. Comfort levels around and between buildings are a function of wind turbulence, and can be improved as a result of built form and proper siting. There are chronic diseases which can be affected by weather conditions, notably heart and circulatory ailments. Although weather, per se, may not be a causal factor, it has the ability to aggravate or ameliorate the course of such ailments.

Differences in social behaviour patterns have frequently been ascribed to climatic influences. Northerners are often described as "cool", while southerners are labelled "fiery". Speculation has created stereotyping that has only recently been receiving scientific scrutiny (Andersen, Lustig & Andersen, 1990). In 1918, R.D. Ward, in the book *Climate: Considered especially in relation to man*, reported that in both the United States and Europe northerners are serious, industrious, enterprising, pessimistic and mature, whereas southerners are cheerful, impulsive, generous, lazy and easy-going. Such characteristics – whether partially accurate or not – have largely been attributed to culture (and its effect on communication) and climate.

Theories have been proposed suggesting that the harsh winters which shaped northern European and Canadian cultures may have encouraged conservative behaviour since life was dangerous and challenging, and too much social arousal and involvement could shift the balance against survival. Ideas have been put forth, for instance, that the reserve found amongst northerners has little to do with genetically conditioned characteristics but rather with learned ones.

This reserve reflects the attempt (most likely at a subconscious level) of northern inhabitants to conserve physical and mental energies which are already taxed by physical environmental stressors. The attempt to "conserve" is echoed in reduced emotional investment and in apparent lack of expression or affect (Heine, 1985).

It becomes clear that linear cause and effect relationships are not simple to identify since most variables can
hypothetically serve as either cause or effect. The environmentally deterministic view believes that physical environment affects behaviour – and cultural norms. Topography
and climate may play important roles but cultural practices
and attitudes can override these factors so that people in the
same environment may display cultural practices which
vary widely (Altman & Chemers, 1980, pp. 10-11). Although
it is held that traditional cultures and the vernacular solutions which they spawned were always ecologically sound
and climatically sensitive, this has not always been the case
– and examples can be found which seem to work badly in
response to climate – reinforcing the sometimes overriding
importance of socio-cultural factors (Rapoport, 1987, p. 263).
This suggests that lifestyle, beliefs, identity and other forces
– together – may be more powerful than climatic ones in the
creation of built form. However, to ignore climate, particularly under harsh conditions, would not be an advisable
course to adopt.

Climatic factors have been ignored or swept under the
rug for far too long. In so doing, there has been a destruction
of both cultural traditions and regionalism in design. Diverse
private interests are replacing public culture which is slowly
disintegrating. Collective well-being no longer seems to be in
the forefront of political concern. If urban design is to be
user-responsive it will have to confront climatic elements
head-on. Design will also have to derive inspiration from
cultural and climatic contexts to instill deep aesthetic and
sensory meaning. A richness which can evolve from a climate-sensitive perspective can assist in heightening the
quality of life. Towns should be conceived to function
equally well in all seasons, and the harsher the conditions
the greater will be the need to pay more attention to climatic
imperatives.

Behavioural Responses to Winter

Anthropologists have generally argued that physical evolution to the stage of *homo sapiens* took place in warm, temperate climates. This "thermal paradise" exerted minimal climatic stress on humans and once this stage was reached, humans were able to migrate throughout the world to places with far less hospitable climatic conditions (Matus, 1988, p. 10). Human culture, acting as a buffer between people and adverse environmental pressures, was thus created.

The main change brought about by the buffering effect of culture was susceptibility to illness or death caused by hostile climates. Some anthropologists have suggested that natural selection ceased to play a predominant role in the evolution of the human species since culture interceded between humans and their climatic environments (Hurlich, 1976, p. 9).

However, precise and detailed information concerning human physiological and psychological response in winter cities is not readily available in a format suited to practical application. Most research concerning human needs in cold climate environments has been carried out in laboratory settings and there is a lack of knowledge about such needs within the context of everyday life. Furthermore, most laboratory work has focussed on assessing indoor comfort in order to develop heating, ventilating and air-conditioning standards and technology, while outdoor comfort research has been virtually ignored. The research assessing indoor comfort has shown that it is difficult to separate physiological from psychological factors since comfort is related to subjective experience.

The main theoretical interpretations of psychological response to winter conditions is that winter causes a downward shift in the ratio of positive to negative psychological stimuli (Persinger, 1980, p. 297). Simply put, there are fewer things for people to enjoy in winter than in summer.

According to Persinger, this occurs due to four main reasons. Firstly, there is an increase in stressful events related to extremes in cold, snow and wind factors. For example, travel may become dangerous, vehicles may break down, and public utility services may fail. Secondly, there is a reduction of readily available recreational activities for most people. Thirdly, the reduced variety in colour, sound, and smell in nature means that most people suffer from perceptual monotony and sensory deprivation. Finally, when people are confined to their homes due to hazardous and inclement weather, they develop "cabin fever" and have an overwhelming urge to escape from their involuntary confinement. The temporary psychic relief provided by alcohol and drugs is often used and abused as an alternative to changes in physical environment.

The main population groups that are susceptible to increased psychological stress in winter are the elderly, normal young to middle-aged people who are prone to depression, and the mentally ill. The elderly are more likely to suffer in winter because of their involuntary confinement due to dangerous outdoor conditions. Normal young to middle-aged people who are prone to depression may lapse into severe depression in winter due to the trigger effect of decreased positive stimuli. The mentally ill may suffer more in winter due to a reduction in spontaneous social contacts because of a decrease in outdoor public activity and an absence of bright, comforting colours (Persinger, 1980, p. 299). If more intense levels of social interaction are desired – when people tend to be confined indoors – proximity and density will be important factors influencing such contact, thereby contributing to a reduction of stress and isolation (Pressman, 1990/91, p. 765).

Winter has a profound impact on social activity in urban environments despite the fact that relatively little research has been executed in this area. It is important to stress two important points. Firstly, the nature of social activity is quite different in winter than in summer. Secondly, the quality and extent of social activity in winter can be improved through planning and design.

Pioneering research in the observation of social behaviour in the outdoors during winter was carried out by Jeffrey Nash, a sociologist from Minneapolis. Dr. Nash used participant observation techniques to determine how people's public behaviour changed in winter. He and his research associates logged hundreds of hours observing public outdoor life in Minneapolis. Based on these observations, they were able to arrive at three general conclusions (Nash, 1986):

1. There is a significant reduction in the use of public space (both indoors and outdoors) during the winter months.

2. There is a sense of festivity in the attitudes of those involved in public life that is often accompanied by extraordinary weather occasions (e.g. heavy snowfalls).

3. There is greater freedom to define appropriate usages of public space in winter.

The number of people using public space in winter probably decreases due to two reasons. During winter, it is often difficult and uncomfortable to travel and thus people are less likely to leave their homes and workplaces. Furthermore, it is often uncomfortable to spend more time than absolutely necessary out of doors. In winter, there are virtually no people who "hang out"; people out-of-doors always seem to have a definite purpose or activity.

Recently, scientists have identified a psychological condition which is directly related to winter climatic conditions.

Seasonal Affective Disorder (SAD) is caused by changes in photoperiodicity (the day-night cycle) during winter, as the amount and intensity of sunlight is reduced at high latitude locations. Sufferers from SAD experience depression at the outset of winter due to changes in two distinct biological systems. Reduction of the duration and intensity of daylight affects secretion of the hormone melatonin which, in turn, depresses mood and subjective energy levels. The secretion of the neurotransmitter serotonin, which regulates a person's appetite for carbohydrate-rich foods, is also affected (Wurtmann and Wurtmann, 1989, pp. 68-75).

Sufferers of SAD complain of periodic bouts of depression with a profound craving for carbohydrate-rich foods. They tend to go to bed early, sleeping for nine to ten hours and their sleep is intermittent and not fully refreshing. Researchers have shown that the incidence of SAD is positively related to latitude. In the northern states of the U.S.A. the incidence of SAD is approximately 100 per 100,000 people while in the southern states it is only 6 per 100,000 people. It is, furthermore, thought that these results underestimate the actual incidence of SAD (Wurtmann and Wurtmann, 1989, op.cit.).

Since insufficient exposure to sunlight has been identified (extensive studies have been carried out in Finland) as the major cause of SAD, phototherapy is being used as a treatment. This involves exposing patients to full spectrum bright light for a few hours a day, and has been common practice in schools located in northern Russia. Many patients have recovered or have had their depression alleviated using this technique.

It is highly probable that most people living in high latitude locations suffer from SAD, at least to a minor degree. Therefore, depression could be relieved by obtaining maximum exposure to sunlight during winter months. This can be achieved by regularly taking part in daytime outdoor activities and, as well, by placing desks in offices next to windows – especially those which are south-facing (Boyles, 1988, pp. 105-107). To prevent a high incidence of SAD in the urban environment, planners and designers should ensure adequate provision of outdoor recreation facilities and adequate natural lighting in indoor working and living spaces.

In light of some of the recent findings pertaining to the effects of northern climates on health and behaviour, planners of winter cities must ensure that urban culture evolves in a direction whereby human physiological and psychological well-being is optimized. In this manner, the health of individuals can be improved and the evolutionary potential of the human species will be strengthened.

TOWARD AN URBAN DESIGN FOCUS

"Urban Design" (often conveyed through many diverse forms and expressions) has resurfaced as a concept and practice at a timely point in the evolution of city planning and urban development. Its purpose is to serve as a means of alleviating dissatisfaction with contemporary approaches to city building and urban planning. Conventional patterns of city planning have often tended to reinforce a 'consumption' rather than a 'conserving' ethic; and a 'reactive' rather than a 'pro-active' approach.

In a social context, conventional practice (oriented towards private development) often fails to adequately represent the public realm; from an economic standpoint, neoclassical models of planning based on market forces and land values displace people and separate work from home; and from a physical vantage, current practices corrupt the natural landscape, threaten the existence of ecological habitats, and consume vast amounts of invaluable natural and agricultural resources. Such approaches are nearing obsolescence, thus necessitating innovative courses of action.

Whereby planning tends to be oriented towards management and policy, urban design translates policy into three-dimensional built form and urban space. Historically, town planning embodied "urban design". Unhealthy urban conditions that resulted from uncontrolled forms of development, industrial growth, and low quality housing, gave rise to the emergence of the "physical planner" or "master planner".

Concerned individuals, with visions of how to improve the built environment, responded to inner-city problems by concentrating on the physical form of cities, addressing the deterioration of living conditions, and the increasingly appalling appearance of towns and urban regions.

In the 19th and early 20th centuries, Ebenezer Howard, Robert Owen, Charles Fourier, and Le Corbusier, among others, represented the "planners" of the day who made decisions and had complete control over them on the basis of their social ideals and technical expertise. Resentment with these old models, failure to address citizens' needs and concerns, and dissatisfaction with this type of planning necessitated new approaches which placed emphasis on public participation and political support. Thus, old-style 'planning' based solely on autocratic models became inapplicable and inappropriate in contemporary society, as it was incapable of upholding the democratic institutions upon which modern planning is presumably based. While this outdated view of planning is capable of threatening democracy, and the public interest that design was meant to address, the role of the 'physical' planner is not obsolete. The urban designer must operate within a democratic framework, but this need not hinder performance or progress. Physically-based approaches to problem-solving are highly capable of responding to the environmental, social, and economic challenges which confront our cities. In fact, urban design can and shall be partially responsible for improving our built environments. Especially in high latitude regions, or areas where unpleasant winter conditions prevail, innovative urban design is a basic necessity which, until recently, has been almost entirely overlooked.

Urban Design in a Winter Context

Unquestionably, architects, landscape architects, and planners have been attempting to redefine city-building in order to address contemporary physical, social, political, economic, and environmental concerns. Leon Krier's masterplan for 'Dorchester', in the United Kingdom (commissioned by the Prince of Wales), and Andres Duany's 'Seaside' in Florida, among other urban projects, are two highly praised examples demonstrative of this trend. Despite such progress these examples cannot possibly represent models to be emulated within all geographic regions. Surely, all cities of the globe cannot realistically embody enough uniform characteristics so as to justify duplication.

Careful application is the key to good design. How to apply city building principles to places entrenched within diverse contextual and climatic settings is the fundamental question. Thus, cities in countries such as Canada, Russia, Iceland, Finland, Norway, Sweden and parts of the United States need to adopt approaches which reflect their specific climatic conditions. To ignore winter's presence is both irresponsible and unreasonable. In applying what is commonly referred to as "neo-traditional" community design, sensitivity will be required since every region imposes its own seasonal demands:

> Building a Neo-Traditional community in Tromsø, Norway based upon a neighbourhood in Florida (where neo-traditional community design originated) would eventually create a situation akin to the one that NTCD (Neo-Traditional Community Design) was developed to rectify. The successful NTCD-based cold climate community would take into account factors such as: protection from the elements; snow and management; optimisation of solar energy; and protecting continuity of access (Hanen and Liburd, 1993, p. 23).

In adopting and importing urban forms from the south
– public squares, open spaces, treed allées and boulevards –
we are using an architectonic grammar unsuitable for cities
which, for a large part of the year, must contend with conditions of severe wind, frost, ice, snow and bitter temperatures.
The geometric and compositional properties of late-
Renaissance Europe and the Beaux-Arts tradition seem most
inappropriate for cold, snowridden towns and cities.
Therefore, policy analysts, urban planners, developers, and
designers would be wise to re-evaluate their positions when
working in such settings.

Lessons from Vernacular Building Design

The climate in which we live has a tendency to determine
our outlooks and life ways. It sharply influences particular
environments – and their effects – for every type of civilization. Even from the slightest variations in climate one can
witness different kinds of social systems and cultural attributes and these are frequently reflected in architectural styles
and building traditions. Especially when necessity pre-
vailed, people have learned how to protect themselves
against nature and weather systems using ingenuity to turn
their liabilities into assets.

Archetypes commonplace in vernacular building reveal
triumphant solutions both for survival and pleasant living –
varying from one mountain valley to another, from desert to
coastal plain, from the equatorial regions to landscapes
bathed by the midnight sun. Designs and ideas dictated by
climatic and topographical concerns are genuine and
authentic, as they must be if they are to respond meaningfully to human needs, local materials, and natural forces.
They have sought to be the way they must without resorting
to clichés, fashion, or dominant trends in stylistic thought.

Most of the world's major towns, especially at northern latitudes, have been founded on sites – or shores – which are south-facing. It is precisely these southern exposed sides which experienced rapid growth. Many Alpine villages in Switzerland and Austria are seen to have their 'chalet' dwellings similarly aligned, sitting on hillsides, facing south, and looking toward the sunshine in cluster formation. This "Alpine" aesthetic is perceived as a unique conception due to the perfect harmony with the natural conditions. An extremely sophisticated level of "identification" with the natural landscape has been achieved by the built environment.

This type of vernacular or indigenous design has received so much attention of late that it is now seriously considered by many prominent architects and planners as the genesis of new theories influencing urban ideas, forms, and sustainable developments. While much of this tradition may appear arbitrary, what is important is that, without exception, the forms have always been a direct expression of life's functions, satisfying local needs from a culture-specific perspective. The social requirements are almost perfectly integrated within the built form in a manner which makes it difficult to differentiate one from the other – to know which element is to be viewed as "stimulus" and which one as "response". Socio-cultural values, building materials, orientation, climate, and site have been uniquely woven together, simultaneously developing a responsiveness, human scale, diversity, and plastic quality which never cease to stimulate either the senses or the imagination.

There are many examples to be found of "northern vernacular". Built forms such as the *igloo* which insulates its occupants against temperature extremes – a veritable thermal fortress or thermally-sheltered cocoon – is a sort of artificial cave serving to illustrate the case. This dwelling shape or "snow house" responds in an admirable fashion (being completely aerodynamic, with a minimal volume) to a sense of far northern place.

In Iceland, where severe winds and driving rain are more common than heavy snowfall, a typical farm cluster is compact and half-buried for protection against the violent winds. Main frontages face south and possess apertures such as doors and windows. Roofs must insulate thermally and have substantial wind resistance while the use of dark colours on the south-facing facades increases passive solar energy gain (Supic, 1982, p. 343).

Scandinavian farm buildings usually group small-roomed buildings around a central courtyard with an open fireplace in the central dwelling space which radiates warmth to the surrounding living areas. The courtyard enclosure acts as a device creating a favourable micro-climate protected from exterior winds. In Finland, people and animals have lived on a side-by-side basis – in Karelia, animals below and people above, thereby benefiting from the released heat. Swiss farms situated in the Jura mountains are formed of continuous dwellings, under one large roof, with western frontages carefully screened from strong rain-bearing winds. Farms located in the Bernese Oberland have extremely large roof overhangs which shelter the working areas beneath the barns.

We should probably keep a sufficient distance from the nostalgia of the past – from literal interpretations of urban forms and architectural solutions – as we confront future problems. However, we ought to retain a sense of the spirit within which problem-solving was approached in the vernacular tradition. It is within a framework that will blend a mastery over nature and a co-existence with nature that meaningful answers will be discovered.

The subterranean habitations of Natives in Oonalashka
(Aleutian Islands) by John Webber,
(Atlas of Cook's Third Voyage, published 1780).
Source: The Anchorage Museum of History and Art (by permission).

The interior of a subterranean habitation in Oonalashka
(Aleutian Islands) by John Webber,
(Atlas of Cook's Third Voyage, published 1780).
Source: The Anchorage Museum of History and Art (by permission).

The "igloo" which typically incorporates the least surface area enclosing the greatest volume of interior space.

Photo: Malloch Collection, Notman Photographic Archives, McCord Museum of Canadian History (by permission).

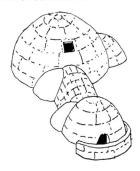

The igloo of the Canadian eastern Arctic.

Source: Building North, Jan./Feb. 1990.

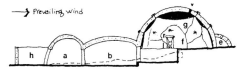

Section and plan of a Baffin Island igloo.

Source: Building North, Jan./Feb. 1990.

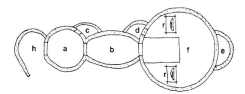

A Typical (Bernese Region) Alpine "Chalet".
Dwelling areas, cowshed, and barn are all grouped under a
common roof. This reduces heat loss, offers protection for the
balconies and working spaces, and shelters the façades from
bad weather.
Source: Milieu Naturel en Architecture, Frédéric Aubry, Lausanne,
Cahier d'information 6-1989/90.

An Icelandic House.
Hugging the ground, these dwellings are covered with sod roofs
providing excellent insulation from the winter cold – an example
of eco-design in traditional architecture.
Source: Frédéric Aubry, Lausanne, op.cit.

Dwellings at Oraefi, Iceland.
At a typical Icelandic farm, earth-sheltered structures are extremely
well insulated with layers of stone and sod covering (20 cms. thick).
Animals stay at the lowest level, with people above.
Source: Milieu Naturel en Architecture, Frédéric Aubry, Lausanne,
Cahier d'information 6-1989/90.

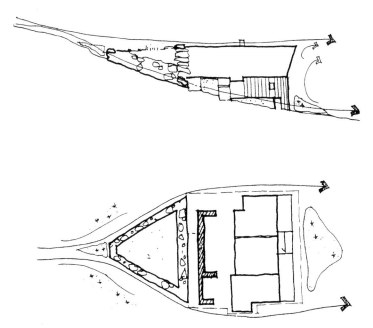

Traditional Building: in the mountain areas of central Europe and in a few places in Norway, houses can be found which have heavy, plough-shaped backs and an open façade toward the sun. Cold air, drifting snow and eventual avalanches are guided around or over these buildings without causing excessive damage. This example is of a "chalet à fort" in Ormonts-Dessus, Switzerland.

Source: Anne Brit Børve, adapted from Plemenka Supic.

Bosco/Gurin (Ticino), Switzerland.

An exemplary vernacular expression whereby a small village is sensitively integrated – in cluster form – with its environs. It represents sustainable development principles which are meticulously adapted to the forces of the site.

Photo: Edizioni Alfa S.A. – 6616 Losone.

Typical Bernese half-timbered farmhouse with strong, protective roof forms.

Photo: N. Pressman.

Grimentz (Valais), Switzerland.
The Alpine chalet turns its back to the cold wind while being exposed to the sun's warmth – embracing dramatic vistas.
Photo: Office du Tourisme, Grimentz.

Ftan, Switzerland (Lower-Engadine/Grisons).

The compact village form embodies human scale and creates a sensitive "fit" with the surrounding environment, preserving it with great care.

Photo: Swiss National Tourist Office.

People and planners living in northern, winter cities have, for a long time, ignored the lengthy and, at times, unbearable winters. Most of the energy of professionals has been focussed on the "warmer" seasons, such as summer, spring, and autumn. Designers have usually not embodied a tradition of basing decisions on seasonal demands. "Thinking winter" was out of the question during the 1950-80 period and prior to that time, as well. However, a genuine "winter-consciousness" has arisen with the inception of the livable "winter cities" movement, created in the mid-1980s, whereby constant efforts at promoting conferences, symposia, discussions and media coverage of "winter problems" were intitiated, and started to make themselves felt in urban policy documents and design concepts in circumpolar regions.

One must adapt to climate and other physical factors which can act either as determining or modifying elements in building and town development. Among all the influences of topographical variations and environmental factors impinging on historically static or living, dynamic urban settlements, the most important one is climate (Egli, 1951, p. 61) – that element which has been most sadly neglected especially in northern situations. The form and structure of northern cities have not been shaped by climatological dictates but rather they have employed technology to render habitable designs and shapes which are fundamentally unsuited to their respective sites and geographical locations. What is essential is that each northern country take advantage of general cold climate solutions with regard to its own conditions.

Providing meaningful developments which are not only functional but also emotionally satisfying is the task which confronts designers, administrators and planners working under conditions where "cold" is a prevailing force. The benefits of designing with nature are not only practical but also aesthetic and sensory. We must learn not only to accept seasonal change but also to appreciate its fundamental beauty. It would appear most appropriate that we consider managing and designing landscapes, buildings and the open spaces between them, in a way which emphasizes rather than minimizes the variation of seasons, in order to create multi-season cities – which accommodate and celebrate life in all seasons.

URBAN DESIGN: THE NORTHERN DIMENSION

Current Dilemmas

Harsh and foreboding climate such as that embodied by northern winters has worked its way into the national psyche of cold nations. Canada, for example, has been imaged by others – and images itself – as a product of climate, to a large degree. Winter has, to a considerable extent, shaped its history, helped to develop its customs and traditions, and has repeatedly been a central theme in both French and Anglo-Canadian poetry, literature, art and other forms of cultural expression.

> For most of us winter has become a rather persistent annoyance that we grudgingly accept but somehow think of as an undeserved plague visited upon us in retribution for an unintended sin (Cavell and Reid, 1988, p. 12).

This generally tends to be the case in other northern societies such as the American midwest, Sweden (particularly its northern regions), Finland, Norway, Iceland, Greenland, Japan's Hokkaido region, and much of the former Soviet Union. The northern bleakness, with its cover of ice and snow and its bone-chilling winds, is deeply embedded in the hearts and souls of those who inhabit the north. On the whole, these cultures work hard at attempting to resist and deny this hostile season. However, at times, they also delight in the snow-reflected light, the visual beauty and the outdoor sports, and festivities made possible by the snow-covered landscape.

The attempts to generate a 'climate-responsive' northern urban form are part of a relatively recent phenomenon and field of investigation. These attempts – and the international winter cities movement – have established the need for explicit, systematic inquiry which analyzes national and local strategic action directed at improving the comfort and lifestyles of northern dwellers. Although there has been a lengthy history of winter living, particularly in rural areas, the literature on this subject has been sparse, lacking emphasis on how to generate solutions for achieving human comfort indoors, out-of-doors, and in that elusive in-between zone of "inside-outside". However, since the emergence of targeted 'winter cities' approaches, and recent case-study literature[1], experience accumulated during the past decade has produced some directions and trends which can now be detected with relative precision.

Legislative norms, administrative frameworks, economic dictates and political priorities – together with stylistic trends and fashions – have been among the most influential forces shaping our built milieu. These factors of international character have been sensitive neither to climatic considerations nor to 'genius loci' attributes. Rather, they have tended to produce buildings and entire neighbourhoods which epitomize "placelessness", as they are so similar in their use of materials, exploitation of site, and isolation from prevailing cultural values. What has resulted is more often a *steady-state*, *thermally-neutral* environment (constant temperature and humidity regardless of natural conditions) where "indoors" and "outdoors" are no longer connected or related. Designs and realizations are similar whether in Oslo or Miami, Toronto or Phoenix, Reykjavik or Los Angeles. The same available technologically-driven solutions are applied, in one case to heat, and in the other to cool, buildings and collective spaces. In fact, the most urgent dilemma of our time is *how to create places which possess genuine meaning* or 'genius loci', in which inhabitants can be proud to reside, and which appear to belong to and spring from their respective geographical and cultural contexts.

This elusive 'genius loci' or the sense of place – imbuing a place with uniqueness – can only occur when three essential human needs are met (Dunin-Woyseth, 1990, p. 341):

> they are the human need for continuity with the past, the need for making a personal impact on the environment and the need for a mutual, balanced relationship with the environment. Considered separately the three needs enhance the approach of fragmentation and specialisation so typical of the immediate past and its characteristic unrestrained growth. Taken together, in a sense of close relationship they contribute to creating places with which people can identify and to which they can feel they belong.

The well-known Québec 'nordicist' Louis-Edmond Hamelin (a human geographer by training) suggested that Canadians lack a true 'collective conscience of nordicity' and that they are "walking to the north backwards with their eyes fixed on their vacations' palm trees". He has often made reference to 3 waves of nordicity in the Canadian mentality (The Globe & Mail, 1988, p. D8):

1. The classic, careless colonial model.

2. A more cautious ecological approach (towards disposing of wastes and protecting animal life, for example).

3. An approach which aims at obtaining the very best in the development of Northern Canada.

It is this last approach and mental attitude which must evolve – in all genuinely northern countries – if we are to retain our most precious legacies, develop life ways which possess harmonious relationships between people and their environment, and if we are to maintain our unique cultural and physical identities. In the face of increasing architectural homogeneity both in Arctic as well as in temperate climates, a special effort will have to be made if a regionally-based, northern urban form is to emerge, which strives to create a true 'sense of place'.

If we wish to optimize exposure to the beneficial aspects of winter, this will demand a creative and innovative approach since there are few positive case studies from which to draw inspiration. Present experience, in most cities throughout the 'winter city' world, has attempted to create "summer city" conditions, throughout the year, instead of highlighting those characteristics which are unique to northern communities.

Interventions in Northern Urban Design Strategies

Urban development policies can be expressed in terms which, on the whole, will tend to remain abstract while identifying long-term goals, aspirations and community images. However, it is essential that such policies be capable of translation into *physical form* if they are to have any meaningful effect. While these forms must be able to meet performance standards (answering the question of what effects are desired), they should also be capable of metamorphosis such that the fundamental design gestures, once implemented, can evolve incrementally into a responsive urban organism receptive to external impulses which cannot be foreseen at the outset. Most of our respected design gestures have withstood the test of time and it merely remains necessary to adapt the best examples from the past (and present) with the intent of achieving *consistency, continuity, functionality,* and *beauty* through purposeful urban forms.

In an attempt to catalogue planning and design interventions likely to become more widespread – based on current ideas in northern thinking – a preliminary list might resemble the following (Pressman, 1993):

I. Visual Environment

a) *Ice as Art*

Ice will be used in more visually stimulating forms such as illuminated fountains, floodlighting of frozen waterfalls, umbrella sprays left from fountains during freezing periods, ice sculpture, and 'snow and ice' decorative features. These can counteract winter's stark qualities – especially at high latitudes – and serve as centre-pieces for civic spaces. Superb examples of polar bears, squirrels and cats made of snow and ice grace the town park and pedestrian street (Storgatan) in downtown Luleå, Sweden.

b) *Use of Bold Colours*

Judicious selection of colours for buildings and public art can provide contrasts under different seasonal variations. The brighter hues – red, orange, yellow – are most easily recognized in daylight and present the highest contrast with snow cover. Skillful planting of coniferous vegetation can introduce colour in landscape and colour 'master' plans can be instituted for polar zones (such as those developed for Longyearbyen on Svalbard by interior-architect Grete Smedal of Norway). Within a colour spectrum and in conditions of changing light, variations

79

become possible making for greater liveliness during day, night and the shifting seasons. Certain colours provide symbolic warmth, literally "heating" space and giving it a warmer, vibrant glow. Others can absorb or reflect light – important factors in winter.

c) *Illumination for the 'dark' periods*
New forms of lighting incorporating intensity, glare, height, shape and clarity factors will emerge. Sodium vapour lighting, for example, tends to be more attractive than mercury vapour lamps during winter. While public safety concerns grow in importance, aesthetic quality cannot be ignored. Log-burning fireplaces have been distributed throughout the city centre in Luleå, Sweden providing both light and warmth – especially effective during the short daylight period. Sun-scoops, reflectors and other devices which bring sun and light into the interiors of buildings are crucial at high latitudes.

d) *Urban Furniture*
Telephone booths, kiosks, public benches, litter bins, bus shelters, planters, newspaper boxes, etc. will become more functional (e.g. less emphasis on vandalproof factors and more on thermal comfort in choice of materials) as well as more visually attractive, thus enlivening both the streetscape and urban space.

e) *Civic Embellishment*
Sculpture, fountains, murals, clocktowers, laser images, banners and flags, signage and other forms of graphic display will emphasize public animation and fantasy in civic space throughout the urban fabric. Visual stimulation, through more intense sensory participation, will add greater vitality to urban life.

Luleå, Sweden – The town's major street (Storgatan) with log-burning fireplaces, which add warmth, and light, to winter. Sidewalks are heated, melting the snow and ice, thus creating a non-slip surface.
Photo: N. Pressman.

Luleå, Sweden – The major shopping street (Storgatan) is a lively pedestrian spine with delightful ice-sculptures reflecting regional themes and exhibiting local character.
Photo: N. Pressman.

Zurich: December on The Bahnhofstrasse – under a dazzling canopy of lights.

Photo: Swiss National Tourist Office.

Getreidegasse, Salzburg (Austria).
A splendid canopy effect is created on the major shopping street by snow clinging to branches strung across the pedestrian space.
Photo: "Cosy-Kunstverlag" Salzburg. Permission by Brigitte David.

*Luleå, Sweden: Snow/ice sculptural slide
in the city centre "town park" (front view).*

Photo: Göran Ström/Municipality of Luleå.

*Luleå, Sweden: Snow/Ice sculptural slide
in the city centre "town park" (rear view).*
Photo: Göran Ström/Municipality of Luleå..

II. Human Comfort

a) *Micro-climatic Studies More Frequent*
   Wind tunnel testing and snow simulations (accumulation and drifting) performed in open channel water flumes will assist in the creation of more tolerable comfort levels for pedestrian-zone activity. Use of the heliodon or computer models can predict sun/shade patterns under varying conditions. (Flour particles and fans can indicate air flows at reduced costs).

b) *Improved Ergonomic Design*
   The elderly, physically challenged, young children, etc. will benefit from improved climate-responsive designs, for instance, of handrails, ramps, stairways, sidewalk curb details. Products such as crampons to prevent slipping on icy surfaces will see larger consumer markets, as will new floorscape materials with non-slip features.

c) *Landscaping Concepts will Reduce Discomfort*
   Selection and location of vegetation, shelterbelts, trees, hedges, walls, fences and orientation of buildings will, in combination, produce better localized climates. Protection from wind and exposure to sun will be promoted.

d) *Ecochart Use will Increase*
   Analytical techniques resulting in mapping systems will plot sunshine and climate parameters (e.g. heating degree days, wind, precipitation, etc.) whose application will assist in more effective site selection and detail development. Detailed knowledge of local conditions will be available and accessible.

III. Protective Urban Devices

a) *Above-Grade Protection*
Skywalk/skyway systems (+15s) and covered pedestrian bridges will be built in carefully selected parts of the city. Calgary, Alberta is an excellent example of an extensive walkway system.

b) *Below-Grade Protection*
Underground pedestrian concourses, tunnels connected to subway stations and other 'understreet' climate-controlled systems will selectively be implemented. Montreal and Toronto are good illustrations although they siphon some life from city streets.

c) *At-Grade Protection*
Colonnades, canopies, arcades, gallerias and glazed-over spaces, including mid-block pedestrian routes, will facilitate movement throughout a city's central business district. These may be linked both to above-grade and below-grade protective systems.

d) *Sidewalk Heating*
Will continue to be used where this is cost-efficient and can make use of recycled heat from refuse combustion or district heating plants. Stairs and ramps shall also be heated in dangerous, high-intensity locations. This is a common practice throughout many Swedish and Norwegian towns.

e) *Multi-Use Buildings*
Buildings containing various functions and activities will minimize the need for movement when these can be concentrated in a single structure or group of buildings.

f) *Retractable Roofs*
Devices which automatically open and close by using pre-programmed electronic sensors sensitive to changing

CROSSWALKS.

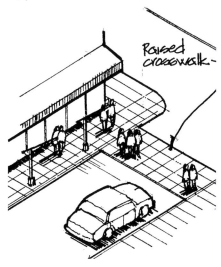

Raised crosswalk -

Suggested crosswalk detail (eliminating curbs) for a typical "winter city".

Source: City of Sault Ste. Marie, Winter Cities Association, and Hough Stansbury Woodland Ltd.: Winter Cities Design Manual.

Electric Snow-Melting System.

Applicable to driveways, walkways, stairs and ramps using small electric heaters and newly developed snow sensors.

Source: Tohoku Electric Power Co. Inc. – Sendai, Miyagi, Japan.

weather conditions may be used not only for sport stadiums but also for central area "main street" shopping and entertainment functions. As they are extremely costly, widespread use is not anticipated.

g) *Pedestrian/Vehicular-free Zones*
Will become more widespread due to increasing concern for environmental quality (air pollution, noise, etc.). During winter – when water, ice and slush are prevalent – with the use of sidewalk heating, comfortably warm, non-slip surfaces for exclusive pedestrian use make more sense than conventional streets. Curbs should also be eliminated at major street intersections and storm sewer inlets re-positioned.

IV. Recreation and Leisure

a) *Parks, Open Space Systems and Waterfronts*
These will be developed more imaginatively using ice, snow, wind and sun as positive features for year-round use. Active participation will be encouraged for all urban inhabitants – from the very young to the very old. Winter as well as summer use is imperative. Interpretive nature programs should focus on winter as well as summer use.

b) *Winter Safari and Wildlife Areas*
These concepts, normally found in more temperate climates, will take on greater importance in urban and regional leisure activities – including tourism. Finland is a leader in this area.

c) *Ski-Trail Networks*
Increasing attention will be accorded to cross-country ski networks within the metropolitan area, for utilitarian and recreational purposes. Trails for physically challenged and blind will be incorporated as will night-use illumi-

nated tracks. (Norway has been the world leader in developing such systems and much can be learned from its experience – in the Oslo metropolitan area alone, more than 200 km of illuminated ski-trails are known to exist).

d) *Winter-Oriented Outdoor Amenities*
   Hockey and ice-skating rinks, slalom tracks, ski-jumps and related amenities will promote 'fitness' and 'sport' programs. Educational programs shall assist in helping young adults to enjoy and appreciate winter life.

e) *Carnivals and Festivals*
   Programmed festivities normally occurring during mid-winter (Winterlude/Bal de Neige in Ottawa-Hull, Québec, Harbin, Sapporo, etc.) and in the pre-Lent period promoting positive images of winter will become more numerous and remain active for lengthier periods.

f) *Winter-Indoor Gardens*
   Climate-controlled parks (which should be intimately connected with the exterior for use in the outdoor season) will be more commonplace incorporating glazed-over, atrium-like structures particularly in far northern regions where prolonged cold temperatures, extensive snowfall and wind, and lengthy darkness prevail. In the majority of cases, they will be situated in public space at ground level, although in some rare instances – such as at Devonian Gardens in Calgary – they may be located 4-5 storeys up-in-the-air in office buildings in the central city.

V. Transportation

a) *Reducing the Necessity to Walk*
   Under adverse conditions, it is desirable to either minimize or entirely eliminate the necessity to be outdoors.

*A typical "spark" or Norwegian kick-sled adapted for summer use
(with wheels).*

Photo: N. Pressman.

*Ottawa-Hull, Canada – Winterlude/Bal de Neige where people enjoy
winter to its fullest.*

Photo: J. P. Fauteux and Ville de Hull.

Skiing Down the Toboggan Slide – Dufferin Terrace, Québec City.
Photo: Notman Photographic Archives, McCord Museum of Canadian History
(by permission).

Skating Rink on Montréal Harbour (c. 1870).
Photo: Notman Photographic Archives, McCord Museum of Canadian History
(by permission).

Rideau Canal, Ottawa, in Winter.
(One of the world's longest skating rinks).
Photo: NCC/CCN – Ottawa.

Ski Trails in
Norwegian Towns.

The 110 year old
"Skiforeningen"
grooms 2,400 kms.
of cross-country
trails in the Greater
Oslo Region
with about 200 kms.
being illuminated.

Photo: Skiforeningen, Oslo.

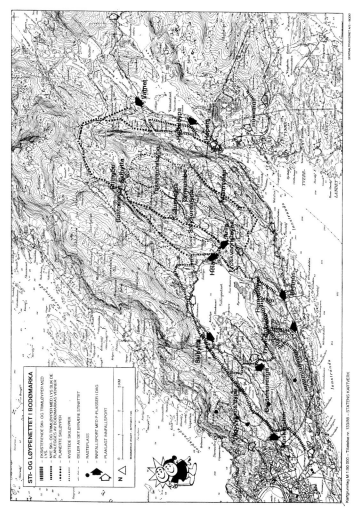

This can be achieved through linked public and semi-private spaces using gallerias, passages, arcades, etc. which run through buildings (used by the public) and between them, offering protection in varying degrees.

b) *Emphasis on Snow Removal*
Effective methods for snow removal and disposal at city-wide and neighbourhood levels will continue to flourish. Snow-melting devices for roof surfaces, sidewalks, drive-ways, roads, and public spaces (Japan is a leader in these developments) will be applied on a broader scale than we have witnessed in the past.

c) *Improved Public Transit*
Bus service will have to shift schedules in response to seasonal demands (more frequent service with shorter waiting times in winter). Better accessibility, especially in suburban areas, will be essential to reduce walking distances and waiting times. Heated shelters are desired at intensively used stops and at interchange stations (from bus to subway/train, etc.). Reduced dependency on the motor car might be worth considering, if accompanied by highly efficient public transit, especially in areas where winters are harsh and lengthy. A healthy balance between land uses (particularly residences and employment) can assist in minimizing travel distances.

To summarize, according to the prevailing trends which are slowly and gradually producing a catalogue of winter-oriented interventions, the most important principle is to *integrate*, rather than isolate, people with their environment. Living *with* winter not in spite of it should be the planners' motto. As Hans Blumenfeld so eloquently wrote:

> Complete exclusion of winter from the city is not a serious option; partial exclusion has to be sought. It can pursue

Engadine Skimarathon at Lake Sils, Switzerland.

On the 2nd Sunday in March, up to 12,000 skiers traverse 42 kms. of cross-country trails from Maloja to Zuoz/S-chanf, the largest annual sport event in the Alps – the way to enjoy winter.

Photo: Swiss National Tourist Office.

Mürren, Switzerland (Bernese Oberland).

One of the numerous "traffic-free" villages situated at an elevation of 1650 metres. With no pollution from cars, an idyllic winter environment can be maintained.

Photo: Swiss National Tourist Office.

two routes, jointly or separately. First, part, but not all of winter's negative aspects can be eliminated throughout the city; second, all can be eliminated from parts of the city (Blumenfeld, 1985, p. 48).

Leitmotifs for Humanistic Design

Despite the intensity of new building activity in the northern-latitude nations, design tendencies generally appear to reflect turmoil rather than consistency. Construction technologies seem to be the most potent sources of inspiration. Major conflicts persist in terms of expression between *organic-regionalism* and *internationalism*, on the one hand, and between *romanticism* and *realism*, on the other hand. A wide spectrum of ideologically rooted approaches has been apparent and is manifested as a kind of 'cultural eclecticism' in the wake of stylistic pluralism embracing elements of *pragmatism, playfulness, vernacular folk tradition,* and an *association of connections* between traditional architectonic and urbanistic concepts spiced with the 'myth of Arctic clarity' (Byggekunst, 1986, pp. N23-N24).

> Stylistic pluralism is by no means the sign of cultural prosperity, happiness, democracy and richness. It results from the confusion of artistic means and categories; it also results from the confusion of artistic and industrial techniques. It results from the destruction of cultural traditions and ethnic identities. Cultural pluralism marks the moment where idiosyncratic private interests and obsessions replace common and public culture (Krier, 1985, p. 57)

Often these conflicting views have as their goal the creation of authenticity which derives from cultural values and emphasizes the unique characteristics of *function* and *place* – the essential conditions for spiritually meaningful art.

Building and space are searching for artistic form which is intimately linked to socio-historical time. They want to 'belong' to their respective environments while simultaneously acknowledging external impulses, thereby seeking a theoretical framework based on phenomenological interpretation. A tension can be sensed between design which springs from *functional pragmatism* and *technological possibilities*, and design which is revelatory and evocative of *place* and *timelessness*. If artistic creation can be viewed as an expression of symbolic intent embodied in material form, then this tension suggests the cultural duality of 'being as having' versus 'being as meaning'. Such dilemmas should be seen positively, for without their existence there would be little dialogue and the essential fuel of intellectual ferment would cease to be present.

Two additional dichotomies further exacerbate the problem of developing a 'grammar for the north'. They are the almost mutually exclusive forces of *privacy* (in dwelling) versus *community,* and *indoor* versus *outdoor* semi-public and public space. The proliferation of single-family detached houses (rather than multi-family forms of collective habitation) are indicative of the former while 'glazed-over' galleria projects are demonstrative of the latter trend towards enclosure. The real challenge confronting urbanism and landscape design under harsh circumstances will be to create an *architecture of 'in-between',* mediating between these opposing propensities, and devising intermediate spaces of climatic and experiential transition.

> Real life takes place in the alternative between life indoors and life outdoors. Thus a double desire appears: to be inside, to be outside ... The satisfaction of this double desire leads to a pleasure, a certain way of regenerating oneself. It seems that this pleasure has not been used consciously in architecture (Sauzet, 1987, p. 60).

The steady erosion of public space and urban place – especially in North American communities – is occurring because local governments are 'bargaining away' civic space for urban redevelopment; making concessions to private developers who are agreeing to provide 'gallerias' which, at best, can only be understood as semi-private or private realm and in which users are allowed access on a selective basis. Private security guards employed by the owners of these shopping gallerias control and monitor all activity – and users – not concerned directly with consumer transactions. Unquestionably, these are private spaces, par excellence, inhibiting the spontaneity which is endemic to genuine public place and civic life. Whatever the reasons for this demise of the public domain, particularly in harsh, climatic circumstances where subtle levels of protection are required – even during the marginal seasons – we require a hierarchy of spatial networks ranging, on the one hand, from enclosed to open-air, and on the other hand, from public to private.

> Between the absolute privacy and the absolute publicity there are (or should be) a number of semi-public possibilities where we can choose our ways and levels of interaction, the momentary balances between anonymity and intimacy, repose and provocation (Torsson 1982).

It has been said that:

> Western philosophy emphasizes deductive reasoning, excluding the senses from the realm of intelligence ... There must, however ... be a balance between reason and intuition for us to experience our environment fully. If we are denied the sensory awareness of temperature variation, the transient qualities of colour and texture in the landscape, changes in natural light, and the inconsistencies of wind movement, the result is a perversely cruel form of isolation – a slow death, one might say (Sandisser, 1985, p. 26).

Swedish artist, Richard Bergh, in 1902 wrote:

It is not so important that all small nations make immediate and astonishing contributions to the great culture ... it is, on the contrary, of major importance that they develop independently and logically from their own roots, working with subjects which especially suit them – in order little by little, and in an original way, to grow part of the larger organism, and address its variety from an original and vital perspective (cited in Nasgaard, 1984, p. 158).

Bergh's ideas were generally accepted by the artistic communities throughout Scandinavia, and Canada as well, but they had little impact upon urbanism or town planning. Except for some brilliant proposals (usually not executed in their entirety) by Ralph Erskine, a uniquely "northern" urbanism can hardly be said to exist. Most professional energy has been directed toward the "warmer" seasons. Designers, on the whole, have not embraced the tradition of "seasonally-based development".

INNOVATIONS IN NORTHERN URBAN DESIGN

New Communities

To comprehend innovative developments based on roughly a decade of recent experience (from 1980-1990) in cold-climate regions, a case study approach would appear to be in order. This will focus on neighbourhood/community planning, often on 'tabula rasa' sites. Such projects tend to emphasize innovative practices — more so than the usual retrofit designs for existing areas. Furthermore, since much of this innovation has occurred throughout the Nordic nations, they will be singled out for their exemplary design and planning.

Most of the projects achieve energy-efficiency (at the building and urban design scale), adopt a climate-sensitive approach, and behave in an environmentally-responsible manner, while espousing the goal of "habitability". Such "habitability" is understood to encompass those qualities of place where residents can thrive and be fulfilled — physically and psychologically — with a minimum of disruption, a minimum of stress and inconvenience, and a maximum of human comfort.

Developing a "Grammar for the North"

One of the pioneers in the field of "northern urbanism" has been architect Ralph Erskine, a long time resident and practitioner in Sweden, of British origin. His work, which has been important in cold climates, has attacked problems at both architectural and urban design/site planning levels. He has suggested that thermally effective designs and concepts not only ought to provide efficiency of performance, but also that they lead to an aesthetic anchored in the characteristics of the various cold regions, thereby producing a vernacular expression which is an authentic outgrowth stemming from natural conditions, and not the importing of forms from more temperate climates – adapted to the rigours of the north through the application of technology.

All of Erskine's buildings and architectural compositions have demonstrated his fundamental ideas. In order to maximize daylight – in climates which, during winter, have long periods of darkness – he has often introduced rooflights and clerestorey windows, frequently with light reflectors which deflect the low rays of the sun toward the central spaces in the structure.

His overall aim has been to develop an adaptable architecture and town design suitable for a range of climatic conditions and client groups, insisting on a participatory process during the design stages. From an architectural stance, Ralph Erskine has been the eminent pioneer calling for a unique approach to northern urbanism. Especially during the 1970s and 1980s, his philosophy has been in harmony with technical, political and economic requirements. It will remain valid throughout the 1990s, as well. He can be said to personify the Zeitgeist of our time:

> Ralph Erskine seems to capture all the pre-occupations of the moment: lowrise, high density, a modicum of participation, an informal aesthetic, a village scale, mixture of new and old, a resettlement of the existing community, semi-private space, ad hoc use of materials, moderate price, etc. If there is a Zeitgeist of the moment then Erskine is she (Architectural Design, 1977, p. 86).

Erskine's most radical innovation for cold climate design is the "windscreen building" or "long-wall", where a slab-like building (usually several storeys in height) is wrapped around the northern perimeter of the building site protecting elements situated within the "wall" (open space, community facilities, playgrounds or low-rise dwellings) from northern winds thereby providing micro-climatic shelter on the sunny orientation – and at the same time, protection from noise pollution from any roadways at the site's periphery. Applications of this important principle have been best illustrated at Svappavaara, Sweden and Fermont, Québec.

Fermont, Québec

The most important project in which the Erskinian "wind-screen principle" has been applied is at the Northern Québec town of Fermont, a resource-based company town of some 5,000 inhabitants, designed by the Montreal firm of Desnoyers and Schoenauer. The development of the planning and design for this town commenced in January 1970. Construction began in 1971 and by 1976 development of the townsite was largely completed. Here, the "long wall" contains the functions of a typical town centre. Along an "interior street" are to be found the library, school, administrative facilities, shops and recreation services. In addition, within the linear, climate-controlled building are found a hotel, indoor swimming pool, bowling alleys and related community equipment.

> In Fermont, a linear five-storey multi-purpose windscreen building was designed to give protection from the cold north-western, northern, and north-eastern winds. According to calculations based on tests, the wind shadow of this 50 foot high building affects the micro-climate of

almost two-thirds of the townsite area. Since the density of dwelling units per acre is higher in the residential precincts affected by the windscreen building's influence, a much larger proportion of Fermont's inhabitants benefit from the wind abatement. In fact, every resident enjoys some protection from the wind because strategically located wide bands of the existing black spruce forest have been retained to shelter all low-density residential precincts (Schoenauer, 1977, p. 6).

Svappavaara, Sweden

The plan organization at Svappavaara (near Kiruna, in the Swedish arctic) employed extremely lengthy three storey windscreen buildings sited at the top of a south-facing slope linked at their bases by community oriented facilities and sheltering housing clusters, within their embrace, which are also south-facing. The town centre facilities were distributed throughout the ground level of the "long buildings" preceding the Fermont scheme by approximately a decade. Unfortunately, the Svappavaara plan was not built in its entirety and those components which were only partially executed have been severely compromised – with but a small portion of the windscreen buildings constructed (without the urban centre) and a much greater dispersed layout than initially intended.

However, the plan of Svappavaara and the writings of its author, Ralph Erskine, have had an influence on Canadian planning for northern settlement. His advocacy of a design approach which combines protection from the elements with a positive experience of the natural environment and which skilfully balances the demands of community and privacy, has universal applicability as a principle for northern towns (van Ginkel, 1976, p. 305).

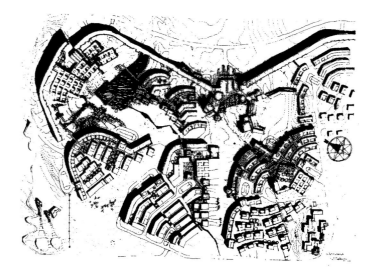

Original Plan of Svappavaara, Sweden (designed by Ralph Erskine).
Source: New Communities in Canada – Contact, University of Waterloo, 1976, p.305.

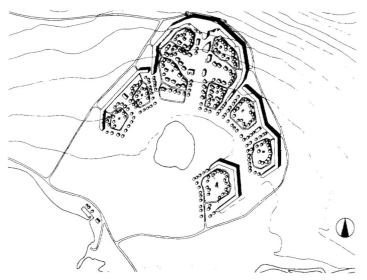

Original Plan of Resolute Bay, N.W.T. (designed by Ralph Erskine).
Source: New Communities in Canada – Contact, University of Waterloo, 1976, p.306.

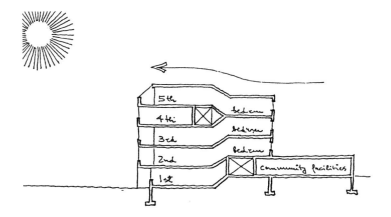

Fermont, Québec – Cross-section of the windscreen building.

Source: Norbert Schoenauer, architect.

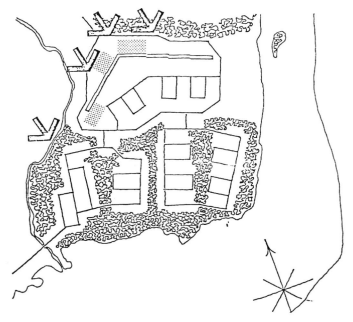

Fermont, Québec – Site plan indicating predominant winds and windbreaks.

Source: Norbert Schoenauer, architect.

Fermont, Québec.
Windscreen building at top protects the town from fierce northern winds.
Photo: Norbert Schoenauer.

Fermont, Québec.
View of the windscreen building from the row housing protected by its "wall".
Photo: Norbert Schoenauer.

A town plan for Resolute Bay, (never completed) in Canada's Northwest Territories, in the early 1970s, accommodating about 1200 inhabitants was deeply influenced by Erskine's planning principles.

Kista, Husby and Akalla – Sweden

Sweden's post-war land development policies resulted in regional strategies which acquired international renown. The first of these "new generation" planned suburbs was Vallingby, west of Stockholm. Although over 30 years old, it is still hailed as one of the most successful ever built. It was known as the first ABC-suburb in the Stockholm region (Arbete or Work, Bostad or Residence, Centrum or Centre). These were intended to be more self-sufficient than earlier housing estates in terms of shopping, and employment opportunities, and more densely structured than earlier housing developments. The overall organization of the ABC community was one which had an underground transit station and urban centre in the middle, apartment and high-density units within a 500 metre radius of the "centre" and lower-density units (semi-detached, row housing and single-family dwellings) situated between a 500-1000 metre radius of the town's centre. Separation of vehicular, pedestrian and bicycle movements was commonplace.

The second generation of new towns, known as the Skarholmen group, included traffic safety (minimization of grade-level crossings by pedestrians) as one of the main features. Although self-containment was still sought, a significant degree of commuting to work nevertheless occurred, contrary to planning goals and expectations.

Kista, Husby and Akalla, a triad of newly planned communities for the North Järva district of Greater Stockholm was drawn up in 1969, and ratified in 1971 with the greater part of the residential and ancillary functions (commercial centre, places of employment, etc.) constructed between 1973-82. These are among the most recently planned communities in the Greater Stockholm region. Close to 30,000 inhabitants reside in these three adjacent communities, linked to one another, from the outset. In Kista there are roughly 3,500 dwellings, in Husby, about 4,700 dwellings and in Akalla about 4,100 dwellings – a total of 12,300 dwelling units.

The housing mix includes multi-family dwellings, single-family houses and pensioners' housing broken down, according to the master plan, as follows (Municipality of Stockholm, 1983, pp. 8-15):

1-2 storey buildings: 32% of dwellings (2,000 are small houses and ground-attached units)

3-6 storey buildings: 46% of dwellings

9-13 storey buildings: 22% of dwellings

It was expected that over 20,000 jobs would be present in the planning district after the service facilities and employment areas were completed. Many large technology-based firms moved to the area and it was anticipated that close to half of the residents would work near their place of residence. The rest would commute by rapid transit to the Greater Stockholm area, including its centre and sub-centres. Travel times by the "underground system" to the central Stockholm station are between 16-20 minutes (12.2 - 14.3 km). The unique features of these communities are the following (Municipality of Stockholm, 1983, pp. 8-15):

1. The 3 were planned and developed simultaneously, each having an underground transit station, a town

centre, a range of housing types, with industrial employment areas within walking distance of the residential precincts.

2. The plans envisaged highly concentrated development (of 850 hectares, 250 are zoned for work, 200 for housing areas, 330 for recreational areas and about 70 for traffic-related uses).

3. A maximum walking radius of 500 metres has been standardized from one's residence to the underground station located at the centre.

4. The pedestrian network is a continuous system running in several directions and crosses all roads and major local streets at grade-separated crossings.

5. In the housing precincts, pedestrian walkways are designed as hard-surfaced "malls" between buildings while "park-type" footpaths have been laid out in the recreational zones and open spaces.

6. It is possible to reach by bicycle or on foot, all community facilities and employment areas within each of the communities. There is the rapid transit and a bus system – as well as a road network – linking the developments.

7. All outdoor park and recreation areas are within easy reach of housing areas. Walking, cycling and even cross-country skiing are the dominant movement modes.

8. Most buildings which envisaged changing functions over time (such as schools, day nurseries, service centres and some playgrounds and parking areas) were designed to be flexibly used and sited centrally in a "service band" running through the districts.

9. The built-up areas and the transport systems have been carefully integrated to obtain a clear and consistent urban structure with straightforward traffic separation.

10. The rather dense, built-up area was kept within tight boundaries and a clear line was drawn between urban development and the recreational areas.

11. In each centre, a community building for cultural and municipal activities is located alongside the residential pensioners' hotels and the senior level school. In this way, various users' needs of assembly rooms, meals services (from the school cafeteria), libraries, leisure facilities, meeting premises for associations, etc. can be accommodated with a minimum of exposure to the outdoor environment, should one opt for such a choice.

12. The shopping centre (of which Kista Centre is the largest) is an "interior street" linking the residential and work zones and containing the transit station with two entrances – one at either end. The shops are located on each side of the "mall" between the entrances to the underground stations.

13. Roads with fairly high traffic volumes are located in deep cuts, enabling pedestrian movements to cross over them in grade-separated fashion, but always at ground level, without having to use either underpasses or overpasses.

14. The employment of district heating systems and the use of pneumatic refuse conveyor (PNC) systems in residential areas have reduced the quantities of trucks, vans and service vehicles in local streets. The PNC installation in Husby and Akalla consists of 16 km of piping and serves approximately 8,000 dwelling units. The

installation in Kista comprises 6.5 km of piping serving some 3,000 dwellings, including 200 single-family houses.

15. Technical infrastructure is provided through two tunnel systems, blasted out of the bedrock. One contains water, electricity and telephone lines while the other is for storm and waste water. Cost and implementation studies have justified this approach.

Most of the inhabitants live in well-equipped accommodation close to commercial, industrial and social services. Walking, cycling and other forms of non-vehicular movement tend to be the preferred modes. Public transit linking the new suburbs and the central city is one of the main features. At the district level, those who live in single-family or other lower density forms of dwelling pay the price of lengthier journeys and a reduced quality of services which are too costly to support in such development. Reliance on the car becomes imperative in such situations. Finally, municipal expenditures for capital costs and maintenance of roads and infrastructure, are important factors in the urban pattern. Energy conservation and related issues tend to be the most dominant forces working toward concentrated development.

Malminkartano (Finland) and Skarpnäck (Sweden)

Both Malminkartano (Helsinki) and Skarpnäck (Stockholm) lie about 10 kilometres from their respective city centres. Both are situated in the intermediate zone between the inner city and the so-called "forest towns" that sprung up after World War II. Both areas are located next to commuter rail lines. They were thought of as a "natural" extension of the urban structure and are "new satellite towns", for approximately 10,000 inhabitants each. Malminkartano and Skarpnäck resemble one another in that both were built on "greenfield" sites and were completed in the mid/late 1980s. The following is a summary of the most important conceptual design principles for Malminkartano and Skarpnäck (Pressman, 1991).

Mixed Activities

The desire to mix activities in a residential area can be seen as a criticism of "bedroom suburb" construction and, in a wider sense, of the entire functionalistic view of the city. "Mixing" was primarily defended on the grounds that it could create "genuinely urban city space". Other grounds were the reduced need for traffic and lower energy consumption. At a very early stage, the goal of mixing workplaces and housing, mainly along the pedestrian routes, became the most prominent design principle for Malminkartano. This principle was also introduced in Skarpnäck at the master plan phase, and for the same reasons: to do away with "bedroom suburbs".

The Social Environment

The identity of the residential block and group of dwellings was emphasized. In Skarpnäck this was realized as the return to closed courtyard-style apartment blocks. In Malminkartano, jobs in offices and small industry and common external spaces were emphasized as a way of providing enriching contacts between occupants. Experiments with so-called "residents' democracy" were conducted in both areas. An experimental project was launched in Malminkartano to improve the cooperation between inhabitants and to increase their chances of having an impact on matters concerning them.

Micro-neighbourhood

On the basis of the research and surveys for the master plan, the Skarpnäck residential blocks largely assumed the form of four-storey, relatively large closed blocks. Thus block courtyards became spatially "room-like" and quite enclosed. Each residential block in the area housed only its own services such as parking (separate building), daycare centre, meeting facilities, etc. The courtyard was further divided into smaller semi-private yards and the stairwell units of most blocks were intended to form a "micro-neighbourhood".

Malminkartano is structurally different from Skarpnäck in that it is a "cluster suburb" whose residential blocks are more distinctly unique in shape and architecture from one another. Planning principles have been consciously or unconsciously made use of in the design of the residential blocks. They include: a) Arrangement of the block into smaller distinguishable groups of dwellings; b) Articulation of the outdoor space according to various occupant groups' needs; c) Locating common facilities alongside daily travelled routes.

Micro-climate

The four-storey enclosed block is ideal for the purposes of improving the micro-climate under Scandinavian conditions. The block's "cold" sides, facing north and east, are accordingly closed and the southwestern side is opened to allow the sun to shine in. A completely closed structure is to be avoided due to the problems related to the drifting of snow. Skarpnäck is an example of such a "partially broken" closed block. Tight Scandinavian building regulations that contain stipulations on lighting angles and distances prevent totally unacceptable or extremely closed solutions. They require that each dwelling is to have an outdoor area (balcony, terrace, etc.) that is to face a "warm" direction (between south and west).

Malminkartano blocks were extensively studied in a wind tunnel through scale models during the planning phase to determine wind patterns. Extra planted areas and trellises, fences and balconies between buildings were suggested technical solutions to contain winds and snow drifts. Proper orientation of buildings was most important. Some blocks were intended to resemble terraced houses and many protective structural elements such as open shelters, pergolas, and glassed-in patios were extensively used, especially on the warm sides.

The curvature of the streets and, especially the pedestrian routes, has been justified as reducing the need for wind-protected passages. The organic, curvilinear and protective shapes of the squares also improve the micro-climate.

Public Outdoor Areas
Both Malminkartano and Skarpnäck paid serious attention to public outdoor areas between buildings. In Malminkartano, public buildings clearly demarcate the central square (Puustellinaukio). Designers of streets, traffic and parks were involved at the preliminary phase. Scale models were used to ensure that the materials and colours of buildings and the square matched. The planning was aimed at joining the buildings and the intermediate spaces into "seamless" wholes. Arcades and canopies are widely used in Malminkartano to connect buildings with outdoor space.

In Skarpnäck, the public outdoor area comprises the central avenue, the square and the central park. The character of Skarpnäck's public facilities is more urbane throughout and their form is more regular and distinct. The square is enclosed by buildings on all sides, and the park area is clearly definable. Similarly, in Ekerö Centrum (near Drottningholm), designed by Erskine, a human-scaled mixed-use development, built between 1984-1990, includes

Plan of Skarpnäck (satellite community), Greater Stockholm Region.
Source: Building Stockholm, op.cit., p.63.
(Architects: Leif Blomquist and Eva Henström/Stockholm City Planning Office).

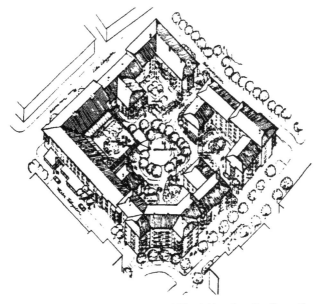

Skarpnäck: Axonometric of Courtyard Block Housing Configuration.

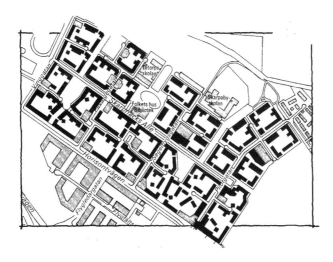

Plan of Skarpnäck (satellite community), Greater Stockholm Region.

Source: Building Stockholm, Swedish Council for Building Research, Stockholm, 1986, p.63.

(Architects: Leif Blomquist and Eva Henström/Stockholm City Planning Office).

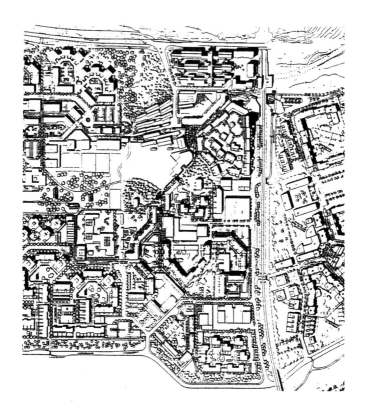

Malminkartano (Finland) Central Area Plan: 1:4000.
Source: Innovative Prototypes for Cold-Climate Neighbourhoods (N. Pressman), 1991.

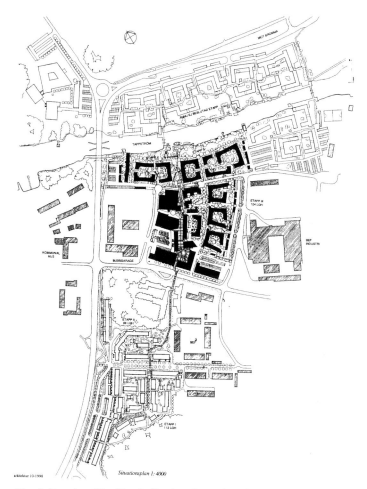

Ekerö, Sweden: Site Plan indicating the pedestrian-scaled streets, squares, and residential courtyards (architect: Ralph Erskine).

Source: Ralph Erskine, Architect, Drottningholm (Sweden)

Ekerö, Sweden – The "village centre" with shops, dwellings, and public spaces all designed to a human scale, near Drottningholm (architect: Ralph Erskine).

Photo: N. Pressman.

Malminkartano, Finland: The windscreen buildings protect a south-facing courtyard with space for play and gardening (architect: Ralph Erskine).

Photo: N. Pressman.

Länsi-Pasila, Finland: typical residential area in a newly planned community outside Helsinki based on medium-density, mid-rise buildings within a "forest" setting.

Photo: N. Pressman.

Länsi-Pasila, Finland: pedestrian walkway within the housing estate.

Photo: N. Pressman.

Skarpnäck, Sweden: courtyard space during winter includes playful architectural forms.

Photo: N. Pressman.

Skarpnäck, Sweden: aerial view along the 'main street' axis.

Photo: N. Pressman.

Kista, Sweden: the grade-separated movement system keeps pedestrians at "ground-level" while cars are below grade.
Photo: N. Pressman.

Kista, Sweden: pedestrian movement spine, with pleasant vistas, is always free from traffic.
Photo: N. Pressman.

parking, post office, church, multi-purpose hall, cultural centre, library, shops, restaurants, public square and 533 apartments applying warm pastel colours to the facades and balconies.

Everyday life in modern cities has become fragmented as work has been further separated from home, traditional neighbourhoods have been demolished or gentrified, and both young and old alike have been institutionalized. Modern urban planning has contributed to this fragmentation by segregating different land uses and functions in an attempt to create a healthier environment and a more efficient urban form. Technological innovation, particularly in transportation and communications, freed people from their ties to a specific locality and thus decreased their levels of social intimacy. Some of the newer Nordic approaches to community design have tried to compensate for these tendencies by bringing back a more heterogeneous mix of people and activities through developing compact, integrated planned neighbourhoods where residents have access to many essential services and facilities and where the creation of an "intermediate social level" involves the activities of household work, care-giving, and local self-management (Krantz, 1988, pp. 7-10).

The Bo i Nord-Arctic Housing Exposition, Norway

During the summer of 1990, Tromsø, Norway hosted the Arctic Housing Exposition. This is part of a series of expositions whose goals have been to generate innovation in housing design, and to demonstrate optimal adaptation of housing and urban design to the rigorous Arctic and sub-Arctic climates found throughout Norway. The site selected was several kilometres outside the centre of Tromsø. The

Norwegian State Housing Bank, The Ministry of Petroleum and Energy, and the Municipality of Tromsø were the key partners. The critical basic guidelines developed for builders, site planners and architects for the "Bo i Nord" exposition – to which they had to adhere – were innovative and deserve careful scrutiny. The main contents included the following (Bertheussen, 1992, pp. 141-142):

1. Sun Conditions

a) Existing access to sunshine should be fully utilized.

b) Common outdoor recreation areas must have access to at least 4 hours of sunshine per day between 9 a.m. and 5 p.m. during the equinoxes.

c) Private outdoor areas should be placed in and faced towards the direction which offers the most afternoon and evening sunshine during the summer season.

d) The kitchen and living rooms must be located so that they together have access to at least 4 hours of sunshine per day during the equinoxes.

e) The projects should pay attention to the fact that the midnight sun may be an asset to the area.

2. Wind Conditions

a) Existing vegetation should be retained and protected, as much as possible, to reduce the effect of winds in the area.

b) Vegetation should be relatively dense in order to function as a maximum windbreak.

c) Buildings should not project much above the vegetation and other formations of the terrain.

d) Houses and recreation areas should be constructed on a small scale to reduce wind tunnel effects and wind speed. The height of the buildings should be gradually increased in the same direction as the predominant wind direction (deflecting the wind upward and away from the ground).

e) The effect of cold summer winds from the north should be reduced by developing more or less interconnected buildings as windbreaks towards the north.

f) Create bends in the road network to reduce the effect of wind channeling.

g) Open spaces between houses should not exceed 30 x 30 metres.

3. Snow and Snowdrift

a) Avoid creating open areas in or close to the dwellings, as this may create snowdrift.

b) Create terraced and staggered buildings which will limit and even out wind speed. Snow will pile up where the wind speed is reduced.

c) Avoid buildings which create long, continuous high ridges to the north and east because this will result in large leeward snowdrift towards the north as well as cold, shadowy areas behind the buildings.

d) Use relatively flat roofs, as the wind will clear the snow off easier.

e) Use the wind to get rid of the snow in areas where you do not want it piled up.

4. Snow Clearing and Depositing

a) The snow clearing executed by the municipality must be kept to a minimum. The maximum distance between snow deposits should not exceed 150 metres.

b) Snow deposits must be placed in the sun so that melting in the spring is accelerated.

c) There must be room for small private snow deposits.

d) The access to the individual dwellings should be short in order to reduce snow clearing in front of garages, dustbins, mailboxes and entrances.

5. Energy Consumption

a) The houses must meet with the energy consumption requirements set by the Ministry of Petroleum and Energy, the Energy Division (saving 25% energy).

b) Heated buildings should be more or less cubic to reduce heat emission from exterior walls.

c) Windows should be placed in positions that reduce heat emission. Avoid large glass areas in roofs.

d) Utilize, if possible, solar heat panels as an additional source of heating during the sunny season.

The above guidelines were developed as a benchmark for future Nordic housing and site planning to demonstrate that climatically-adapted, large-scale residential planning is feasible – and indeed, desirable. It has been acknowledged that executive officers and administrators within municipal authorities have had inadequate knowledge in the fields of climatic-adaptation in building and town planning. As a result of this "Bo i Nord" exposition, future urban development within Norway will be extremely difficult without the projects presenting satisfactory documentation (e.g. climatic impact statements) concerning optimal climatic sensitivity – to the demands of the site, and the needs of the inhabitants.

Human Behaviour: We turn our backs to the rain and wind, tuck our heads down, cross our arms and bend our knees. We wear protective clothing which shelters us on the outside and provides freedom of body movement. Buildings should also apply these ideas.

Source: Anne Brit Børve, architect, Oslo.

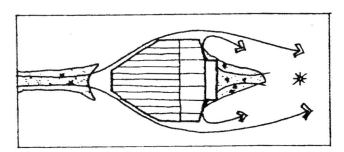

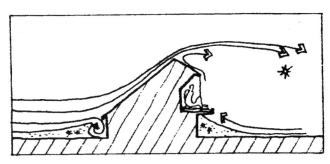

Buildings – A house can have its back to the wind and weather with low walls which guide and direct the wind. A protective overhang shelters the warm, sunny side. Storage and hallways are situated on the cold side while recreation rooms face the sunny direction.

Source: Anne Brit Børve, architect, Oslo.

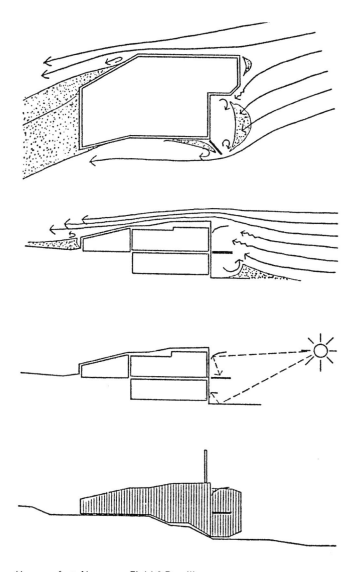

Hammerfest, Norway – Field 6 Dwellings.

Snow, sun and wind conditions, including aerodynamic concepts, influence design. The forms enable buildings to stand out in a landscape covered with drifting snow.

Source: Eilif Bjørge, architect, Bergen.

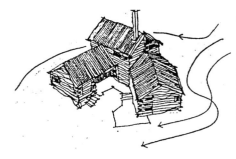

Saxi/Wichstrøm House, Vardø (Norway).

Traditional forms in which the house protects the outdoor area against winds from the east.

Source: Eilif Bjørge, architect, Bergen.

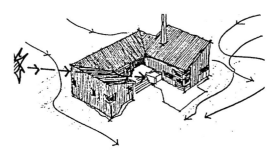

Pedersen House, Vardø (Norway).

High walls offer shelter against winds from the east and north. The outdoor area is bathed in sunshine

Source: Eilif Bjørge, architect, Bergen.

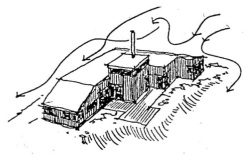

Holmquist House, Vardø (Norway).

High walls face the south to catch the sun. Entrance wall is exposed to the wind for assistance with snow clearing.

Source: Eilif Bjørge, architect, Bergen.

Housing Designs Exhibiting Climate-Responsive Principles.
Source: Eilif Bjørge, architect, Bergen.

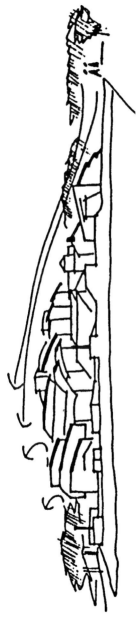

If buildings can be aerodynamic, the entire urban "envelope" can also adopt this principle – deflecting winds over the town and creating improved conditions within its network of streets and public spaces.

Source: Anne Brit Børve & Bo i Nord, Tromsø, 1990.

CANADIAN URBAN DEVELOPMENTS

Canada has been one of the world leaders in responding to harsh, climatic concerns through urban developments situated largely within the central business districts of its large and medium-size cities. Some of the more significant projects will be described herewith as these embody concepts and principles applicable to a broad range of international settings. Furthermore, they are indicative of the fact that the central areas – despite the proliferation of regional shopping centres which are motor car orientated – still serve as the primary foci of employment, government, retailing, entertainment and habitation. Development policies at both municipal and provincial levels have contributed to a strengthening of housing and jobs within easy access to transit-orientated commuting. Without a doubt, such policies are among the prime elements which assist in preserving and enhancing "livability" in many communities, supporting urban vitality. The creation of visually attractive, economically viable, safe, climate-controlled environments – providing for activities and their related spaces throughout all seasons – was the dominant aim.

Toronto's Downtown Underground Pedestrian Mall System

This system is considered to be the largest one of its type in the world (the second largest is Montreal) at present and comprises close to 10 kilometres of interconnected passageways and shopping malls beneath the central city. It came about as a result of the city's subway construction – combined with extremely rapid development in the 1960s and 70s – through both private and public cooperation. This intricate network constitutes close to 500 shops, in excess of 3,000 hotel rooms together with 3 million square metres of office space and residential accommodation. It is a continuous system which is linked to the subway stations, major office structures, key department stores, banks, the city hall, parking garages, the Eaton Centre and Union Station (the main railway station). Development policies for the downtown sector have tended to encourage expansion of this pedestrian mall as new buildings progress with more of the newer sections containing "public areas" with benches, trees, fountains and sculpture. As the Railway lands, south of the city centre, are developed and with Harbourfront (along the edge of Lake Ontario) being expanded, these, too, shall eventually be integrated within the larger subterranean and above-ground spatial framework.

Calgary, Alberta: +15 Pedestrian Walkway System

The +15 (feet), or +5 (metres) walkways are an integral part of Calgary's downtown transportation and open space system. They enable pedestrians to move in climate-controlled walkways and on bridges which are situated at approximately 15 feet above grade or street level, safely separated from vehicles with the added benefit of weather protection. The Calgary system – one of the most extensive of its kind anywhere – boasts over 40 bridges and 10 kilometres of walkways providing access to office, retail and cultural facilities as well as to indoor and outdoor public spaces. In a survey undertaken by the Planning and Building Department, City of Calgary – Development, Land Use and Downtown Division entitled *The +15 System: Pedestrian Counts and a Survey of Users* (October 1986), when asked what the most desirable feature of the system was, respondents' results were thus:

Weather protection was stated as the most desirable feature of the +15 system by 57% of the users. Convenience and separation from traffic ranked significantly lower, 20 percent and 14 percent respectively.

In the 1970 Calgary Plan, "protection from adverse climate" was cited as one of the major objectives of the system. The City decided to go above grade – rather than below grade as in the cases of Montreal and Toronto – because it felt this created a more acceptable walking environment providing improved accessibility to, and easier circulation within, buildings. The +15 plan was integral to a master plan for the entire downtown with the aim of connecting buildings and creating a total pedestrian environment one level above the street – moving through buildings and over open spaces. Bridges are paid for by a combination of public and private funds – often with developers contributing cash-in-lieu of constructing +15 components to the interest bearing +15 Fund since 1971. The City Planning Department negotiates coordinated hours of operation along specific +15 routes with the general rule being openings between:

1. 6:30 – 7:00 a.m. and 2:00 a.m. (when serving evening entertainment).

2. 6:30 – 7:00 a.m. and 5:00 – 6:00 p.m. (when serving office buildings).

Developers, on the whole, manage and maintain the +15 walkways through their buildings and the bridges that they build while agreements obligate the City to assume responsibility for the policing. The City, however, remains the legal owner of the +15 bridges.

There are major American cities such as St. Paul and Minneapolis, in Minnesota, which have huge pedestrian skywalk systems, as well as numerous smaller urban centres in which these can be found, such as Duluth, Sioux City, Cedar Rapids, and Des Moines, to mention but a few.

Devonian Gardens, Calgary

One of Canada's and one of the world's most unique "winter gardens" situated in the centre of a large metropolis is Calgary's Devonian Gardens. It comprises 2.5 acres (approximately 1 hectare) of natural beauty in a fully-enclosed, climatically controlled environment in the heart of the city. Its setting is 46 feet (15 metres) above street level and it is surrounded by shops, offices and restaurants. It contains 138 varieties of greenery including 16,000 Florida tropicals and over 4,000 local plants adorn the pathways which wind past effervescent fountains, sparkling waterfalls, attractive sculpture and wooded bridges. Seating accommodation for 800 persons is provided throughout terraces and public spaces – not to mention the children's playground. There is a skating rink which is transformed into a reflecting pool when the weather is warm, while the "Quiet Garden" and the "Sun Garden" welcome users desiring a spot for peaceful contemplation. Stage and art display areas provide settings for periodical exhibitions, lunch hour concerts and performances.

Admission is entirely free with the hours of opening being 9:00 a.m. until 9:00 p.m. daily.

This indoor park responds to a vital need for passive recreational space during the long, cold winter months when it is clearly inconvenient to use outdoor space in Calgary. Unique is the fact that most of the cost was borne by a private, charitable foundation – the Devonian Group (hence the name) – which contributed $6 million, with the Oxford Development Group (owners of the office development) contributing $4 million, and the City of Calgary supplying a final $1 million.

An average of some 300 events are held annually in this park found four storeys up in a highrise complex – an exceptionally rare urban experience. The developers own both the building and the gardens and lease them to the City of Calgary for $1.00 per year. The City's Parks and Recreation Department provides for administration and maintenance while the developers share security aspects with the Calgary Police Department.

The gardens are considered "public space" but they retain the right to have persons evicted for unruly behaviour. This may or may not cause them to be classified as "semi-private" space. They are a grand success with conservative estimates suggesting that 850,000 people per year enjoy the facilities and skating rink. Guests from virtually every country in the world have been there.

Miscellaneous Examples

The above examples provide some of the leading efforts in climatic protection operating below-grade and above-grade. There are many others which could have been described. The cities of Winnipeg (one of the coldest, large cities in the

world) and Edmonton have a system of combined "+15"
pedestrian bridges and underground pedestrian mall networks woven throughout their central business districts.
Montreal has the second most comprehensive subterranean
pedestrian system rivaling Toronto's. In addition to its
"Place Ville Marie" underground, the north end of the Rue
St. Hubert – in the city's east end – has been canopied where
the shopping function is most intensive (maintenance costs,
normally shared by shopkeepers associations, can be rather
considerable with canopy systems). Kitchener, Ontario has
completed two +15 bridges linking the major downtown
shopping mall – Market Square – to a modern hotel, on one
side, and an office tower on the other, with this complex
connected to a multi-storey parking structure.

The West Edmonton Mall in Edmonton, Alberta, adver-
tised as the "eighth wonder of the world" is a testimony to
how modern technology, coupled with high capital investment, can totally change climate and environment. It is the
single largest shopping mall in the world combined with
entertainment areas, hotels, – and virtually everything
except a hospital and cemetery! This project covers the
equivalent of 24 square city blocks but is located on the
periphery of the metropolitan area thus draining much of the
city's vital energy and robbing it of much-needed sales. It is
especially indicative of the tension existing between "city"
and "suburbs" within the North American context.

Most developments have tended to eliminate climate by
providing increased amounts of interiorized and privatized
space. What remains is to develop micro-climatic outdoor
spaces for public use, particularly during the marginal seasons, whereby users can choose to be in open-air settings
which afford some protection from wind and cold without
having to make the choice of being either "inside" or

"outside". This is the challenge which confronts landscape architects, urban designers and town planners in the future.

During the past two decades, micro-climatic concerns have been emphasized, especially in the central areas of larger cities where redevelopment has been prevalent. In 1979, as an outgrowth of micro-climatic problems, the City of Ottawa approved planning policies intended to address concerns which involved noise, pollution, lack of sunlight between tall buildings and wind turbulence causing pedestrian discomfort. These policies dealing mainly with sunlight access, snow-drifting and accumulation, and wind turbulence control have broken new ground and have contributed significantly to a much more sophisticated urban design approach to development.

In 1987, the City of Winnipeg introduced a special urban design review process. Embodied within this review was the promotion of pedestrian comfort levels based on micro-climatic analyses and evaluation of proposals. Guidelines have been established which have as their objective the raising of standards for downtown development; the introduction of vegetation and colour; and, most importantly, climatic impact statements which study sunlight access, shadow configurations and produce wind tunnel simulation emphasizing snow drifting and wind problems. These characteristics are codified in zoning by-laws thereby providing much more than mere lip-service to outdoor comfort in the city's central business precinct. Additionally, emphasis has been placed on management techniques for encouraging the development of indoor parks and more intensive year-round use of the river embankments throughout the metropolitan area.

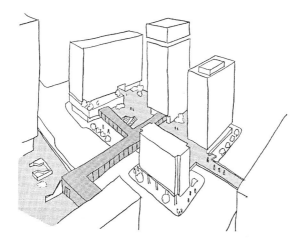

Calgary's +15 pedestrian walkway – Perspective.
Source: City of Calgary, Planning Department.

Calgary's +15 system – View at pedestrian level.
Photo: N. Pressman.

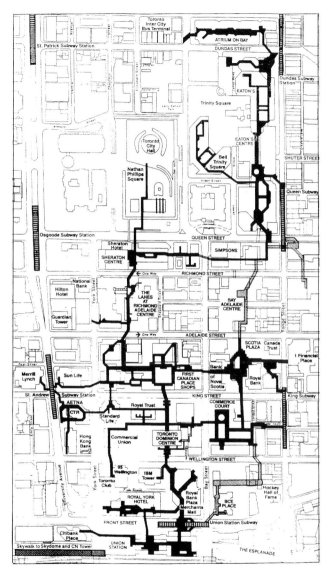

Downtown Underground Pedestrian Mall System, Toronto, Ontario.
Source: City of Toronto, Planning & Development Department.

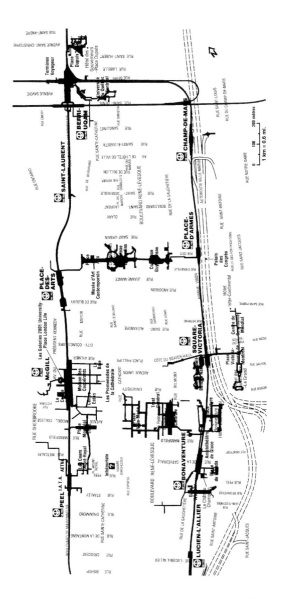

Underground Pedestrian Network (souterrain) – Montréal, Québec.
Source: Ville de Montréal.

A Critique of Underground Concourse Systems and Skywalks

Many cities make proud reference to their underground pedestrian concourses. Usually, but not always, they are linked to metro or subway stations below-grade making separation between vehicles and pedestrians possible. In both Montreal and Toronto, roughly 10 kms. of such walkways currently exist. With the hostile winters and sometimes unpleasant marginal seasons, they have been justified – on the premise of climatic protection – and on the notion of maximizing land-use in the most intensively developed areas of the city's centres. These tend to be the main advantages especially when connections are made to railway stations, parking garages, hotels, large office and shopping complexes, and even to institutional uses (such as the Université du Québec in Montreal – where academic buildings are superimposed on a metro-station). Thus, a continuous and almost self-contained system can be established which attracts fairly heavy use under adverse conditions, as well as throughout the year.

In recent years, the City of Montreal has raised serious questions about the desirability of having such an immense underground (souterrain) which, since its inception in 1962, has come to practically dominate inner-city life at the expense of street-level activity. Although the system largely contributed to the consolidation and dynamism of the central area, its further expansion tends to be seen as a force which can seriously weaken commercial activity, and public safety, on the streets. The magnetism of the underground movement system is assumed to be largely responsible for a decline in the number of retail establishments at street level during a period in which there was an overall increase in the retail sector.

Hence, careful attention must be paid to the overall objectives of a city's development if a balance is to be struck between "street-level" and "underground" activity and whether an "underground" approach should be adopted at all as a form of competition to traditional street life even when vertical separation is deemed desirable due to sidewalk congestion. It is noteworthy that on January 26, 1990, the 10-year master plan for Montreal was unveiled. The major features had as an objective a strong desire to have more people *live downtown* and *shop above-ground*, in comfort. The city also uses zoning regulations which encourage street-level commercial/retail functions and discourage further expansion of the underground.

Similarly, Toronto's underground seemed to be siphoning off street-level vitality. Its underground malls assume a dominant role with respect to street animation in the banking district. Only by exercising great skill in development control can some equilibrium between the two levels be achieved in the urban core.

Skywalks and +15 aerial bridges were intended to separate vehicular from pedestrian flows while providing a network which is safe and efficient throughout the downtown core – linking the most heavily travelled zones. Not unlike the underground concourses, skywalks have also drained some business from street-level shops. The long-term result of unbridled skywalk expansion is normally a single-purpose city centre comprised of high-rent office blocks, department stores, luxury hotels and multi-storey parking structures connected one storey above the street. The only solution for alleviating this condition is to restrict skywalks to particular zones and to make sure that they do not grow beyond a managable size – constantly monitoring their impacts on ground-level activities. However, it should be pointed out that connected skywalks have managed, rather successfully, to compete with suburban shopping malls that, in North America, have often drained retail functions from the central city.

The most successful examples are those in which sky-walk development is balanced by viable, outdoor streets and public places. Calgary's 8th Avenue pedestrian mall acts as a counter-thrust to the powerful pull of its more than 40 aerial bridges, covering a total of nearly 10 kms. By creating multi-level shopping enclaves within large buildings (preferably well-connected to the street through careful design), and invoking policies that keep retail functions at street level, an equilibrium can be reached. Its up-in-the-air walkways can be viewed as much more than simply a series of bridges link-ing buildings. In addition to the convenience (especially during cold periods), comfort and safety, they open up new attitudes to integrating conflicting activities so that these support each other and create a new urban dynamic.

Critics of skywalks are becoming more numerous as these systems are seen (especially in the U.S.A.) basically as providing ultra-convenient shopping and working places but not much else. Some even think they are symbols of urban abandonment rather than reinvigoration relegating the street mostly to automobiles, instead of to people. Perhaps sky-walks can be justified in extremely high-density cores such as those in Tokyo where the sheer numbers of pedestrians and vehicles require a movement hierarchy. Maybe they can play a role in areas of extremely harsh climate. The truly important question to raise is whether the density of most of today's cities can satisfactorily support two or more systems of movement which compete with one another (Lehrman, 1988, pp. 10-11).

Each northern city will have to develop a framework – within its public mechanisms and policies – for developing criteria capable of answering the question "what is a good city?"". Preservation of the historic architectural tissue, the creation of multi-functional public spaces, connections between these spaces and other imagable places, linked via pedestrian pathways, including cultural, administrative and leisure "magnets" all combine to generate a livable and dynamic *city centre* – quite distinct from a central business district where purchasing power counts most.

Copenhagen's success with its public streets and spaces is largely due to the fact that the gradual transition of uses has been publicly-sponsored. The squares and streets of the medieval core, now largely free of vehicles, can be compared to the "theatre" where the streets serve the function of a stage. An alternative way of imagining them would be akin to an "urban beach" on a pleasant day. The dictum of "people attracting people" is explicitly demonstrated whereby those free, public joys of urban life are made available to all who wish to participate.

Like a gigantic party, people return frequently and linger when they are having a good time. The mix of functions and people, the attractive window displays so characteristic of Danish shops, the concerts, street-theatre, parades, carnivals, and places to eat and drink – all contribute to making the centre a highly desirable version of the "urban beach". Although going to the beach is decidedly not a winter activity, with good micro-climatic conditions,the city centre can become attractive during the marginal seasons – and especially in summer. One of the ways to compensate for winter confinement, says Danish architect Jan Gehl, is to make summer conditions very attractive, so that public life can flourish to its fullest. A good winter city, therefore, must also embrace all of the qualities which enable summer activities to be thoroughly exploited.

With the shift toward greater private investment in core areas, public amenities, enjoyed by all social groups using the city, are endangered. As Jan Gehl has repeatedly mentioned (Gehl, 1989, p. 8):

> Traditional public open spaces have contemporary counterparts: shopping malls, arcades and atriums, festival markets, underground cities, and skywalk systems. The innovations have tended to concentrate urban life in certain locations, certain hours, and certain categories of "acceptable" activities. These spaces are mostly indoors and nearly always privately controlled offering privatized versions of the once public street life.

The important issue is to ensure that public policy envisages a state of equilibrium between collective concerns and private interests. New projects generate incremental privatization, resulting in traditional users being displaced elsewhere to find locations which meet their needs. This dilemma can be offset by opening up more genuinely public space – parks, streets, lanes, alleys, squares, and green-areas. Public life for everyone must be viewed as a legitimate concern of local and national authorities.

CLIMATE-PROTECTED STREETS
AND PEDESTRIAN SPACES

Streets and public urban spaces should be carefully integrated within a city's urban tissue and must not be treated as residual elements or spaces left over after planning. These should form an essential component of the urban structure, be clearly connected to important functions, and possess symbolic representation with sharply defined "identity".

In extreme climatic conditions, some climate-protected space will be essential. When providing such protection, it is imperative that the open channels of the streets and public urban spaces retain their dominant roles (even though occasional aerial walkways or skywalks, and underground concourses may be incorporated).

An excellent example of 'galleria-type' climate-protected pedestrian movement can be seen in Hamburg's impressive "Passagen-viertel". Here, seven constructed passages (of which the Hanse-Viertel is the best known) are combined within the "fussgängerzone" (pedestrian precinct) comprised of open-air, car-free streets, and the Colonnaden (built in 1877). Together, there are roughly 1.2 Kms. of interiorized passages running through existing buildings within the city centre, meshed with approximately the same length of pedestrian streets resulting in a choice for users of being either indoors or outdoors – or both, depending on the weather and the season. Hamburg boasts more arcades (passagen) than any other major city in Germany – nine in total, dating from the 19th and 20th centuries. These include hotels, shops, restaurants, coffee-houses, and department stores woven into the historic fabric of buildings and public spaces along the riverbank of the Alster. As early as the 19th century, the Alster Arcades were completed. They allowed people to stroll, eat, shop and meet friends totally protected from inclement weather (rain or occasional snow). The "Passagen" are viewed as part of Hamburg's activities of walking, gazing in shop-displays, and spending free time.

Today, its city centre illustrates precisely how the combination of enclosed (privately developed) arcades can be integrated with the city's network of public streets to produce a high-quality environment for inhabitants and visitors alike. In this large metropolis with an underground subway system, there was no need to introduce above-grade or below-ground paths replacing the traditional street system. In the town's heart, people have been accorded priority over vehicles without resorting to any vertical separation.

Although weather protection is not generally considered to be a major problem throughout Germany, many German cities have been adopting an approach which protects pedestrians – mainly from precipitation, in centrally located shopping zones. In Hamburg, overhead canopies continuously shelter people by projecting over the sidewalks from buildings to which they are attached. In September 1989, the City of Wilhelmshaven, situated on the cold, windy North Sea close to Bremen, sponsored a competition for a continuous system of galleries (arcades), canopies and passagen to be connected within the pedestrian zone and to the peripheral parking areas. The idea was to create what are called "Trockene Wege"(dry paths) making walking and cycling more pleasant, comfortable and attractive. This project has not yet been fully built and is still under construction. However, an already completely realized landmark development occurred in the city centre of Bremen – the Lloyd Passage – which incorporates the "glazing-over" of one of the most important pedestrian shopping streets. It is now the most intensively used shopping street in the central zone.

Some Swiss cities, notably Zurich, Geneva, Lucerne, and Bern have employed underground movement systems for pedestrians in specific locations such as those connecting the main-line railway stations to major pedestrian thoroughfares beneath the railway station "squares" around which heavy motorized traffic exists. An example is the Shopville-Bahnhof passage linking Zurich's Hauptbahnhof (main railway station) with the Bahnhofstrasse "transit-mall" (for pedestrians, tramways, taxis and emergency vehicles). In Bern there is also a below-grade shopping centre connecting the busy railway station beneath the the Bahnhofplatz to the Neuengasse.

Bern is a particularly noteworthy example of climate-protection from wind, rain and snow. The "Lauben" or linear arcades/colonnades which run the entire length of this ancient city's major streets (raised slightly above the roadway) are integrated with the extremely well preserved 17th and 18th century houses under which they are incorporated (the city having been founded in 1191). Within this network of "arcaded" streets accommodating pedestrians and cars alike, mid-block, covered cross-connections and open-air narrow lanes and alleys link the arcades of parallel streets within the old town. Newer "passagen" were skilfully built within the older network. Many are heated with infra-red lamps during winter creating desirable micro-climatic conditions both in the mid-block connections and within the arcades themselves. Year-round use for cafés, snackbars, and even vendors' stalls is possible, and is maintained to a large degree.

If one were to adopt, as an index of pedestrian comfort, the ratio between the total length of protected pedestrian ways and the number of inhabitants, then Bern (having roughly 8 Kms. of weather-protected walkways) with some 300,000 regional population has about 1 Km./37,500 inhabitants of climatic protection. The City of Calgary, Alberta, with the largest +15 skywalk system in the world, and its 600,000 population supports 10 Kms. of protected aerial walkways, or 1 Km per 60,000 inhabitants.

If only the actual "urban" population of Bern were used (135,000), then the ratio of protected ways would increase to 1 Km./16,875 persons probably making it the most completely climate-protected system anywhere in the world – certainly unsurpassed anywhere in extent or importance north of the Alps. The "Lauben" of Bern are a living testimony of how arcades can play a truly significant role in the organization of town form and the use of urban space.

The design principles embodied in the arcades of Bern – and in other Swiss Zähringer new towns such as Murten, Thun, and Fribourg – in its old town, are superb examples of how old ideas can, in the present era, structure daily life and have retail behaviour adjust to an historically imposed urban form. Bern is dynamic and full of vitality while offering diverse activities. It continues to maintain a pedestrian-oriented, vehicular-accessible shopping area and generally has an exemplary mix of uses, including basement cellars for small theatres (Beckman & Ackerknecht, 1994, p. 57).

Its "old town" has been classified as a 'world cultural landmark' and is protected under a UNESCO conservation order. The centre has direct access to the centrally located railway station and, as well, makes provision for huge underground parking garages with electronic panels displaying information about how many available spaces exist in the city's various parking areas.

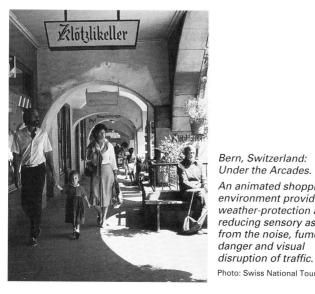

Bern, Switzerland:
Under the Arcades.

An animated shopping environment providing weather-protection and reducing sensory assault from the noise, fumes, danger and visual disruption of traffic.

Photo: Swiss National Tourist Office.

Bern, Switzerland: The Kramgasse with its arcades and fountains has the Zytgloggeturm (clock tower) as a focal point.

Photo: Swiss National Tourist Office.

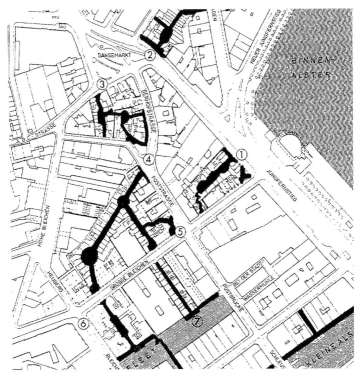

"Passagen-Viertel" (Arcade District), Hamburg, Germany.
Source: Climate-Sensitive Urban Space (Boudewijn Bach/Norman Pressman),
Publicatieburo, Delft University of Technology, 1992, p.34 and City of Hamburg.

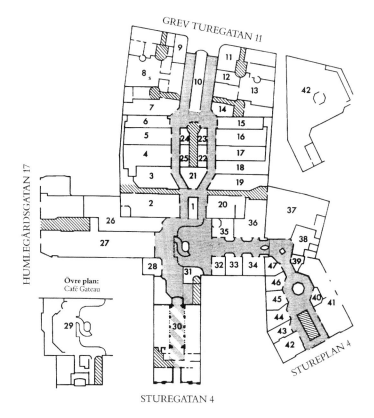

Stockholm: Sture Gallerian, with its many urban "tentacles" wedged in between Stureplan and Grev Turegatan, one of the city's large redevelopment blocks.

Source: publicity brochure.

Vlissingen, The Netherlands – St. Jacobspassage.

An existing pedestrian street, which has been glazed over, in the core of a small southern Dutch town, creates elegance and comfort for inhabitants and visitors.

Photo: N. Pressman.

Annecy, France – Quai Fleuri du Thiou in the old town.
Continuous awnings provide effective, low-cost weather protection.
Photo: N. Pressman.

Salzburg, Austria – In one of the town's public squares (Alter Markt), a
canopy of umbrellas provides the simplest form of climatic protection.
Photo: N. Pressman.

*The Hague, The Netherlands – A heavily glazed sidewalk café
(McDonald's) in the city centre where one feels both "inside" and
"outside". Infra-red heaters provide a comfortable environment
during cold winter days.*

Photo: N. Pressman.

*Bern: The Von Werdt-Passage built in the late 19th century still
remains one of the city's vital "interior streets". Close to the railway
station, it houses an interesting mix of clothing, food and book shops,
pharmacy, and cafés – exerting a powerful attraction.*

Photo: N. Pressman.

Although historic examples cannot readily provide instant solutions to contemporary dilemmas, they can offer guidelines and valuable insights which will serve as a basis for new directions – even when these are little more than the modification of older, time-tested responses. The relationships between *density, weather-protection, mixed-land use, the dense network of public transport, accommodation of the car, compactness, and climate-protected pedestrian movement systems,* can all be witnessed in Bern's urban structure. This city performs well – within its centuries old container – even when evaluated by the most modern performance standards. Most importantly, it still serves as a potent prototype for inner-city redevelopment plans and proposals, although some concern has been expressed that residential functions are being displaced by retail, office and institutional uses (Beckman and Ackerknecht, 1994, op.cit.).

Modern planners, engineers and urban designers would be well advised to analyze this exemplary case-study. There are probably more lessons to be learned here than from many "post-modern" approaches to creating humanized public space. The "internal-external" urbanism has been produced without resorting to vertical separation such as aerial skywalks or underground systems which often tend to compete with safe, animated street-level urban life. Finally, all new buildings or renovations in Bern must conform to the high-quality historic urban fabric, through the application of rigorous building controls.

SUN, WIND, AND SNOW CONTROL

Consulting engineering firms, especially in Canada (but also in Norway, Finland and other northern countries), have been among the pioneers to develop techniques related to the study of existing or potential wind, snow, pollution and sun/shade problems associated with a broad range of development projects – industrial, commercial, residential, through to university campus master plans and planned communities. They utilize open channel water flumes and a boundary layer wind tunnel for analysis of such projects as snow control studies for town sites; wind pressure and aeroelastic studies for high-rise structures; pedestrian level wind studies for open spaces and publicly exposed plazas; studies of exterior shadowing and daylighting; and other research relying on hydraulic engineering techniques applied to urban development projects.

The most significant work tends to be applied to pedestrian level wind studies – conducted to help architects overcome high velocity, and sometimes dangerous, wind conditions which normally occur at the ground level and adjacent to the facades of tall buildings – and to controlling snow drifting, particularly around building entrances and on rural roads, highways, and airport runways.

High winter winds and snow drifting in intensively used areas can be controlled through several methods. Windbreaks and shelter belts can protect buildings, roads, and green open areas from such winds. Specifically designed fences can be utilized for wind protection in places where windbreaks and shelterbelts cannot be planted. Both natural vegetation (shelterbelts and windbreaks) and fences can be used to prevent snow drifting on exposed roads. Long multiple-storey buildings located perpendicular to the predominant winter winds can also be used as windscreens to protect lower density structures or open spaces situated on the leeward side of the winds.

Wind Flow Interactions with Buildings

Wind and buildings (whether tall or of medium height) interact with one another producing wind flow patterns which can create uncomfortable conditions. For instance, the exposure to prevailing winds will normally dictate how windy the area around a building's base will be, since high wind speeds and gusts are generated at the base. This can be alleviated by positioning buildings correctly on their sites, relating them carefully with respect to neighbouring structures or by applying remedial measures. It is imperative to understand the following wind flow characteristics, if comfortable conditions are to be the result of proper urban design (Rowan Williams Davies & Irwin Inc.,1991):

1. When wind meets a building, some of the wind flows down the building face, causing accelerated wind speeds at the windward corners.

2. Terraced or stepped buildings will gradually break up approaching wind flows.

3. Low buildings create a low wind pressure area immediately downwind, and when located upwind of a tall building, they cause notably accelerated wind speeds at the windward corners of the tall building.

4. Alignment of elongated buildings with, for example, prevailing westerly winds, minimizes impact on wind flows. Cutting or chamfering windward building corners further reduces impact.

5. An open passageway through a building creates windy conditions inside the passageway and reduces the sheltered condition behind the building. This effect is magnified as height increases. Use of the passageway by pedestrians will be uncomfortable.

6. Wind flowing at an angle to a long and tall building is concentrated at the downwind corner. This effect increases with building height and length.

7. Non-pedestrian podiums facing prevailing winds retain stronger wind flows and provide reduced wind activity on walkways around tall buildings.

8. Wind which funnels between two buildings causes accelerated winds (wind canyon effect).

9. Buildings can be used as windscreens but pedestrian areas should be carefully selected. Doors or sidewalks should be avoided near the windswept building corners.

10. Canopies or podiums are beneficial on the windward face. Parapet walls will make the canopy or podium more effective. Pedestrians should have a choice of being protected (on cold days) and being exposed to windy areas (on hot days).

11. Pedestrians should have a choice of calm or windy areas through the use of building arcades.

12. Partially enclosed walkways must be oriented to consider the prevailing wind directions, and winds influenced by nearby buildings.

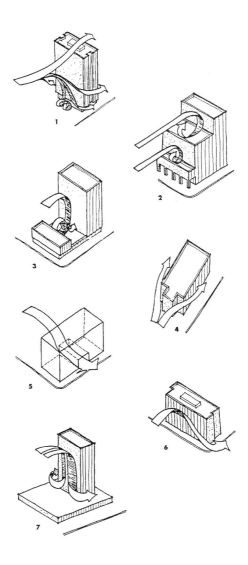

Reference Wind Flow Diagrams.
Source: Rowan Williams Davies & Irwin Inc., Guelph, Ontario, engineers.

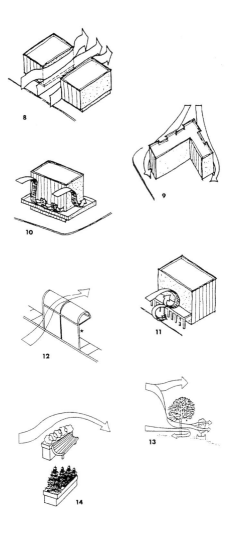

Reference Wind Flow Diagrams.
Source: Rowan Williams Davies & Irwin Inc., Guelph, Ontario, engineers.

13. Underplanting will assist deciduous trees in providing ground level wind protection, but should not be used where wind flow beneath the tree canopy is desired.

14. Small scale features such as benches, planters, and lattice screens should be placed to shelter pedestrians from adverse wind conditions.

Windbreaks and Shelterbelts

The following design criteria have been suggested for shelterbelts and windbreaks to protect areas of intermediate-scale urban design (Caborn, 1965; Verge & Williams, 1981; Robinette, 1983):

1. *Placement*
Shelterbelts and windbreaks are most effective when they are placed perpendicular to the prevailing wind.

2. *Height*
Height of trees is probably the most important characteristic, because the distance that protection extends to leeward is proportional to the height of the windbreak. The distance that protection extends is therefore expressed in windbreak heights.

3. *Density*
Density of different height levels in windbreaks is important for wind reduction. It is also a consideration in terms of the amount of time required for effective wind protection (as trees grow to their mature heights).

4. *Length and Width*
Length and width of windbreaks are only important insofar as they affect density. Making windbreaks wider than necessary to achieve moderate density has no added effect on

wind reduction. In general, windbreaks patterned on multiple rows produce maximum desired foliage density at all levels.

5. *Configuration*

The configuration of windbreaks affects the degree of wind reduction and penetration. Shelterbelts with a pitched roof cross-section are the least effective at stopping wind and should be avoided. The most effective windbreak configuration is an irregular one which is more effective in reducing eddying than a uniform one.

The advantage of vegetation windbreaks and shelterbelts is the fact that the vegetation filters the wind without attempting to deflect or stop it entirely. Air which passes over the top does not sweep down to the ground and resumes its normal pattern some distance downwind. Air which passes through the belt emerges on its leeward side at a slower velocity.

It is suggested that large scale windbreaks and shelterbelts are more effective when they are long (i.e. ten times the height of the trees). Windbreaks and shelterbelts can reduce wind velocity by 40% over horizontal distances up to four times the height of the windbreak or shelterbelt. Thus, long and tall windbreaks can provide effective wind protection for fairly sizeable developments, such as housing projects, mixed-use areas, or children's playgrounds.

The benefits of planting extensive windbreaks and shelterbelts, especially in areas which receive intensive use, go beyond the wind control aspect. They provide aesthetic value as well as good natural habitat for flora and fauna. However, their use, in urban areas, may be limited due to lack of available land as well as by the fact that dense and non-transparent planting in open spaces are often undesirable due to security and human safety considerations.

Fences for Wind Control

Where vegetation cannot be provided for controlling winter winds, fences and physical barriers can provide an effective, although somewhat expensive solution. Four types of fences can be used for wind protection:

1. Solid.

2. Solid with slanted baffles.

3. Permeable with horizontal louvres.

4. Permeable with vertical laths.

Solid fences are often ineffective windbreaks as they try to stop wind thus creating problems of eddying and swirling. In general, they should not be used as windbreaks except under localized conditions and where a high degree of wind shelter is required. Solid barriers with sloping baffles prevent wind turbulence since the baffle directs the wind upwards in a gentle arc. When the baffle is sloped away from the wind, a large protected area is created. Fences with horizontal louvres tilted upwards away from the wind are a good solution for areas where wind velocities have to be reduced, but where ventilation must be maintained. Fences with vertical laths provide the best wind protection at a distance of three times the height of the fence on the leeward side and thus provide good shelter for larger areas.

These fence designs can be used to reduce wind speeds in built-up areas if the heights are carefully designated. If noise barriers are necessary to protect residential zones from vehicular noise, those barriers that are perpendicular to prevailing winds can also be used for wind protection through design modifications such as the addition of baffles.

Where there are wind problems due to downdrafts from tall buildings, for example in residential areas, wind protection can be provided through various means, such as arcading the street level at the sidewalk, or by providing overhead structures such as overhangs and canopies. In general, such problems can be minimized, for instance, by placing tall structures with the long axis parallel to prevailing winter winds or by bevelling the corners of the structures.

Snow Drift Control on Roads

Snow accumulation on roads can cause high degrees of discomfort by preventing or complicating vehicular access. This problem can be alleviated in situations where there is a high degree of snow drifting onto roads. Such situations often occur in areas where roads are directly adjacent to open spaces, such as fields that retain snow which can be readily transported by strong winter winds.

It is possible to reduce snow drifting on roads by raising the road to let the wind sweep it clear, by installing temporary or permanent snow fences, and through planting shelterbelts and windbreaks. Raising the road to let the wind sweep it clear should only be done in situations where there is little or no pedestrian movement, since the increased exposure will make the road uncomfortable in winter for people using it. This strategy is particularly appropriate for arterial roads where pedestrian traffic is not anticipated.

The installation of temporary snow fences in critical areas during winter is an inexpensive strategy that can be applied to almost any setting. Permeable snow fences have been found to be more effective than solid fences for accumulating snow. In general, the snow fence should be placed between 15 to 30 times the barrier's height upwind from the area to be protected in order to provide sufficient space for snow accumulation. The placement of a snow fence, relative to the area to be protected, depends upon many factors, such as the size of the open area upwind; the seasonal snowfall; and the local terrain.

Snow fences can be placed in several different configurations to provide drift protection. When the predominant winter winds are perpendicular to the road, the snow fence should be positioned parallel to the road. When winter winds are at an angle to the road, short fences that are perpendicular to the wind and at an angle to the road should be staggered along the road. When winds have variable directions, parallel and staggered fences should be combined to ensure adequate drift protection.

Sometimes, it is appropriate to use vegetative shelterbelts and windbreaks to provide drift protection for roads. This situation occurs where topographic variations that cause turbulence reduce the effectiveness of snow fences. Thus, taller barriers such as vegetative snowbreaks become necessary. These snowbreaks should be more permeable than vegetative windbreaks. In this way, the wind is slowed down and the snow is dropped. If vegetative snowbreaks are too dense, the wind will simply be deflected and the snow will be dropped further downward (Caborn, 1965, p. 193).

Street Layout, Orientation, and Public Seating Areas

Street orientation influences solar access provision. This is particularly important in residential neighbourhoods where solar access to the street as well as to the dwelling units and outdoor living areas should be considered.

Generally speaking, it is preferable to orient as many streets as possible close to an east-west axis in residential zones. This allows for the possibility of guaranteeing solar access to the dwelling units and outdoor living areas while maintaining reasonably short sideyard setbacks along the street frontage (Regional Municipality of Hamilton-Wentworth, 1980, p. 37). It is possible to provide solar access to dwelling units on streets that are oriented on a north-south axis. However, the sideyard setbacks along the street frontage should be wider (resulting in higher infrastructure costs) and the shape of the solar envelope must be modified (Knowles, 1981, p. 22).

Although east-west street alignments are appropriate for providing solar access to dwelling units and outdoor living areas, they can result in the street and sidewalk being shaded for much of the day in winter. This can be avoided by increasing the building setbacks or by reducing building bulk on the south side of the street (The City of Kitchener, Ontario has had such a building by-law in effect for a long time). Overshadowing of streets in residential neighbourhoods should not cause extensive discomfort since they are not used for intensive outdoor activities. However, attention should be paid to streets around intensively used areas such as schools, bus stops, shopping plazas, arenas, and community centres. Solar access should be provided for these areas and zones by ensuring adequate setback and height restrictions on the south side of the street. Stepping buildings back from the street at a 45 degree angle is a common practice.

Alternatively, streets with institutional or commercial uses in residential neighbourhoods can be oriented north-south, or on a 45 degree angle to north (in either direction). A north-south orientation will assure solar access to the street during the noon-hour while a 45 degree angle to the north will assure that at least one part of the street will be sunny during the winter day (Knowles, 1981, p. 21).

Public benches, chairs, and seating areas should always be facing a southerly direction in regions with winter climates. This can be witnessed in most Scandinavian towns and built-up areas. Scandinavians are serious sun-worshippers (due to the high latitudes at which they live and the short periods of daylight they experience in winter). As a result, they are extremely sensitive to all issues dealing with solar access, and this is reflected both in their building codes and traditional patterns of development.

The design of urban furniture, in terms of functionality and selection of materials, is very important for durability and comfort. A city, like a home, has its public furnishings that make it comfortable, aesthetically pleasing and utilitarian – while capable of expressing symbolic values such as "civility" and good taste. Elements such as benches, bus shelters, kiosks, signs, clock-towers, banners, and fountains have the ability to humanize and "soften" urban space. When these elements are sensibly designed and climate-responsive, they make residents and visitors feel more "at home".

An excellent example of public seating design can be seen in the benches, especially conceived for the City of Zurich, located on the Rathausbrücke, linking the left and right banks of the Limmat river. They have easily movable back-supports allowing a swivelling action to occur so that view and orientation can be shifted conveniently over 180 degrees. It is possible to sit either facing south, with a view of the old town, the "Grossmünster" cathedral, and down the Lake of Zurich toward the Glarus Alps, or facing north (away from the sun) to watch passersby and a small market area replete with vendors' stalls accompanied by enticing sights and scents. Although Zurich barely qualifies for the term "winter city", the design of its outdoor public furniture is exemplary for climatic zones far more severe than that which prevails in northern Switzerland – at lake level. Likewise, many of the tram and bus-stop shelters, designed for Basel, exhibit excellent industrial design concepts which

Kungsträdgarden, Stockholm – Benches always face toward the south in a country where sun worship has always been taken seriously.

Photo: N. Pressman.

Zurich, Switzerland – Benches on the Rathausbrücke have movable back-rests offering users the choice of sun or shade orientation accompanied by different vistas.

Photo: N. Pressman.

Standard Public Transit Shelter for the Basel Region.

Prototype of lightness, economy and elegance. In colder areas, greater enclosure can be built, with the potential for overhead heaters.

Source: Fürrer + Fasnacht, architects, Basel.

Photo: Andreas F. Voegelin, Basel.

could be emulated in colder areas by making only minor modifications.

Windscreen Buildings

Windscreen buildings are linear multi-storey structures located with the long axis perpendicular to prevailing winter winds. They usually shelter other low-rise buildings that are located on the leeward side. Windscreen buildings should have the majority of their fenestration and outdoor living areas facing leeward and southward to provide maximum winter comfort. When such buildings enclose an urban space from more than one side, they can also create "sun traps" (e.g. in courtyards) that reflect the sun back into the space they enclose, heating it significantly. This kind of solar access is possible where dominant winter winds blow from the northeast or northwest. In this case, windscreen buildings fulfill solar access criteria if they are located in the northern portions of the site and thus do not overshadow other low-rise buildings. In some geographic locations, predominant winter winds blow from the south. In such cases windscreen buildings are in conflict with solar access design criteria.

When windscreen buildings are built in sub-arctic climates, they provide several benefits. Since the buildings are long and thus cover a fair portion of the site, they can provide internal pedestrian circulation such as in Fermont, Québec where the town's "main street" is located within the windscreen structure. Commercial and recreational facilities can easily be accommodated and accessed, especially by residents living in floors situated above the "interior street" (or below it). This is the equivalent of placing a linear shopping mall within a residential (or mixed-use) building. In very high latitude communities, windscreen buildings located in the northern sections of the site usually provide additional benefits during summer, as they shade the lower-rise buildings of a residential complex from the midnight sun (Zrudlo, 1972, p. 54).

Micro-climatic Improvements for Play Areas

The provision of high-quality micro-climates in children's play areas, especially in neighbourhood planning, is extremely important if the outdoor season is to be extended. Comfortable outdoor play areas are even more important to achieve in winter when children tend to be confined indoors for extensive periods. In winter, children need to be in contact with other children and with the outdoors as frequently as possible. Play areas can be designed for winter activities by ensuring the best possible micro-climatic conditions. Their achievement can be met by applying the following guidelines:

1. Areas of most concentrated winter play activities should be protected from prevailing winter winds. This can be accomplished through the use of mounds, plant materials (especially coniferous trees), fences, buildings, or any combination of these elements. This wind break material should be located on the prevailing wind side of the intended play areas. Appropriate solar exposure during winter may cause excessive solar exposure in summer. This can be avoided by planting deciduous trees which provide summer shade.

2. Warming shelters or highly sheltered areas should be provided for every exposed outdoor zone. If the play area is too cold, surfaces facing toward the sun could be

painted in dark colours making them comfortable to touch. In addition, warming the area with reflected heat is a desirable strategy to employ.

3. Incorporate a convenient water source to flood areas for skating, creating ice-slides, and making snow and ice sculpture.

4. Provide for a variety of snow conditions to facilitate the many forms of play. Softer snow can be created by reflected sun; deep snow by wind breaks; and clear, slippery areas can be blown free of snow by channeling winds. Channeling winds is also a technique for creating interesting snow shapes and changes to the existing land forms.

5. Integrate existing play structures into winter playgrounds by anticipating wind and snow drifting patterns, as well as reflections from the sun. Use of decks from play structures can serve as shelters. (Canada Mortgage & Housing Corporation, 1981, p. 7.2-7.3).

One of the biggest problems with vegetation in parks and playgrounds during winter is the excessive emphasis on formal avenue plantings. Avenue plantings of trees with an open understorey actually increase wind speed by jetting the wind between the crown of the tree and the ground (Caborn, 1965, p. 176). Such formal plantings should be avoided in playgrounds and small parks that are well exposed to approaching winter winds. Where such plantings already exist, wind jetting can be reduced by cutting every alternate tree to reduce the density of the tree crowns, or by underplanting the trees with tall shrubs or hedge-rows that would dampen the wind jetting effect.

The application of windbreaks, shelterbelts, fences, and mounds is especially appropriate for the design of comfortable winter play areas. However, the need for transparent landscaping, for security reasons, may often be an important consideration, particularly when designing for children's needs. Therefore, trade-offs between wind control and security may have to be made when attempting to create comfortable winter playgrounds.

Stockholm, Sweden – South Station Housing: interior courtyards create multi-season conditions for play and leisure.
Photo: N. Pressman.

Seating design need not be elaborate to attract users. Simplicity and economy are usually the best guidelines to follow.
Photo: N. Pressman.

PRINCIPLES FOR CLIMATE-RESPONSIVE URBAN DESIGN

The micro-climate is normally a factor that is unique to each and every development site. Human settlements in the north have usually attempted to "wall out" inhospitable surroundings, wherever possible, through transforming harsh outdoor climate into comfortable indoor environment. Achieving suitable micro-climatic conditions – especially on the site around and between buildings – will undoubtedly enhance the quality of thermal comfort. Therefore, performance standards which protect users from increased wind speeds induced by the design and positioning of buildings should be formulated. They should be combined with measures to guarantee daylighting requirements, proper air circulation, and access to sunlight through the configuration of built form.

Sites should be selected with the most favourable micro-climatic conditions where feasible. Buildings should be designed to reduce wind speeds around them, to improve outdoor comfort, as well as to decrease wind loads and infiltration rates. Effective wind controls require a rigorous site analysis including wind speed, frequency and direction; slopes and vegetation types; and positions of neighbouring structures which can influence the airflow pattern. Dense, tall coniferous trees, carefully planted, often in rows, can act as "wind sponges" or windbreaks and can divert cold wind currents.

The detailed understanding of using "nature to fight nature" – through planting policies – can go a long way toward reducing wind and temperature-induced discomfort. Tools and techniques are readily available for evaluating the impact of adverse climate on urban areas. Open spaces between buildings can be designed for improved micro-climate in cases where it is undesirable to totally enclose or climate-control them.

> In nature, even in farmland, there are marked differences in micro-climate in different topographic, moisture-rich and sun-orientated situations. They are essential to the full experience of a landscape: the windy ridge, the sun-drenched slope, the sleepy hollow. So central to the design of landscapes for pleasure or production, why are they so rarely considered in city design? (Day, 1990, p. 169).

Much is known about how to moderate climate severity and how to extend the outdoor season through use of wind shields, orientation for maximum reception of solar radiation, prevention of shadowing by tall buildings or natural elements, use of heat absorbing or heat reflecting materials or even outdoor heating – such as overhead radiation heaters. The major principles for creating optimum micro-climates in colder, or even temperate, regions which experience some "wintry" conditions include the following (Pihlak, 1983, pp. 34-35):

1. Protection from the wind especially during winter and the marginal seasons of early spring and late autumn.

2. Orientation of buildings and open spaces for reception of maximum solar radiation.

3. Prevention of overshadowing by buildings and natural elements.

4. Utilization of heat absorbing materials for heat retention.

5. Avoidance of cold micro-climatic air pockets.

6. Provision of built form or vegetation as 'windscreen' protection, from prevailing winds.

7. Design of south-facing 'sun pockets' to function as comfortable outdoor gathering areas during the less comfortable seasons, e.g. cool spring and autumn days.

8. Use of canopies, arcades, gallerias, passages, and other overhead shelter systems which cover primary pedestrian movement areas – providing weather protection and retarding outgoing radiation at night.

9. Provision of paved surfaces on south-facing slopes to maximize heat gain from solar radiation.

10. Pruning and thinning of existing shade trees and plants to permit maximum solar penetration.

Some additional general recommendations for improving cold climate design have been suggested (Glaumann, 1990). For example:

– save existing vegetation for provision of wind shelter.

– keep building heights fairly equal and, if possible, not higher than the surrounding landscape and trees to avoid increased windspeeds. Streamlined forms generally have less turbulence.

– small scale buildings and open areas reduce windiness at pedestrian levels.

– do not allow for unduly large snow deposits and place them in sunny locations, providing for drainage.

VEST POCKET PARK.

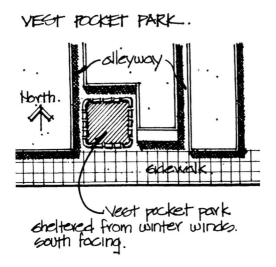

Vest pocket park
sheltered from winter winds.
south facing.

Vest Pocket Park.

Source: City of Sault Ste. Marie, Winter Cities Association: Winter Cities Design Manual.

OUTDOOR ROOMS.

Outdoor Rooms.

The creation of sun pockets and protected space.

Source: City of Sault Ste. Marie, Winter Cities Association: Winter Cities Design Manual.

Pedestrian Walkway.

Canopy over south-facing seating area creates a "lee" effect with conditions which are sheltering.

Source: City of Sault Ste. Marie, Winter Cities Association, and Hough Stansbury Woodland Ltd.:Winter Cities Design Manual.

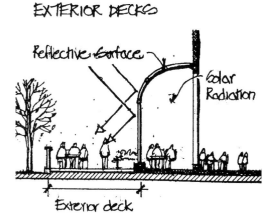

Exterior Decks.

Interior spaces can be linked to desirable exterior micro-climatic spaces for multi-season use.

Source: City of Sault Ste. Marie, Winter Cities Association: Winter Cities Design Manual.

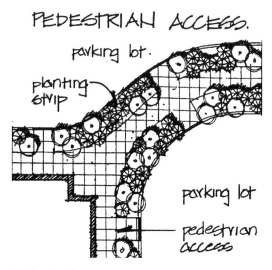

Pedestrian Access.

Pedestrian comfort levels can be significantly enhanced in parking areas by sensitively conceived shelter.

Source: City of Sault Ste. Marie, Winter Cities Association, and Hough Stansbury Woodland Ltd.: Winter Cities Design Manual.

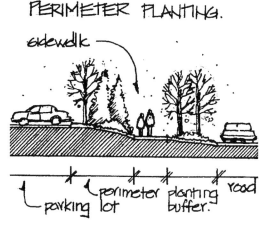

Perimeter Planting.

Buffers protect pedestrians.

Source: City of Sault Ste. Marie, Winter Cities Association, and Hough Stansbury Woodland Ltd.: Winter Cities Design Manual.

SNOW DRIFTS.

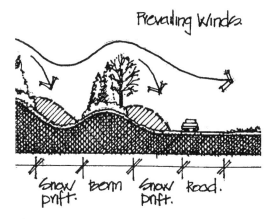

Prevailing Winds

Snow drift. Berm. Snow drift. Road.

Snow Drifts.

Properly designed berming allows collection of snow away from roads.

Source: City of Sault Ste. Marie, Winter Cities Association, and Hough Stansbury Woodland Ltd.: Winter Cities Design Manual.

SETBACKS OF LANDSCAPE BUFFER.

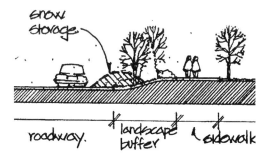

Snow storage.

roadway. landscape buffer sidewalk

Setbacks of Landscape Buffer.

Snow storage requirements should be accommodated by landscape buffers.

Source: City of Sault Ste. Marie, Winter Cities Association, and Hough Stansbury Woodland Ltd.: Winter Cities Design Manual.

SUMMER USE

trail - walking , cycling.

WINTER USE.

trail - cross-country skiing

Trail Systems.

Trails for recreational or utilitarian purposes should optimally be used for summer (walking, cycling) and winter (cross-country skiing) seasons, as well as during the marginal periods.

Source: City of Sault Ste. Marie, Winter Cities Association, and Hough Stansbury Woodland Ltd.: Winter Cities Design Manual.

- make private walkways short to reduce snow-shovelling and minimize distances to mail-boxes, garbage bins, garages, etc.

- make roof inclination rather low to avoid uneven snow loads.

- place walkways and intensively-used outdoor areas out of reach of sliding snow or ice.

- avoid using outdoor, unprotected stairways.

- heated buildings should preferably use compact shapes to reduce heat loss.

- make use of active solar collection and passive solar gain, wherever possible.

Although northern living implies spending much time indoors due to inclement weather conditions, it is nevertheless imperative that attention be directed toward the exterior appearance of buildings and public spaces, not only because they can be seen from the inside but also because they constitute an easily recognizable, positive framework around social contacts all year long, serving as a common focus of identification (Smedal, 1992, p. 103). It might be said, in general, that most Canadian towns have hardly used colour to counteract the drabness of winter, while in many communities in northern Norway and Sweden, colour has been used for a long time with the effect of brightening building surfaces. A west-facing facade of rust or cadmium yellow, for instance, toward sunset, creates a magnificent effect with the late afternoon sun providing a warm, almost magical glow on the building, accompanied by light reflected off of the surrounding snowy landscape.

The Norwegian writer, Andre Bjerke, stated that "nature never makes a mistake with colours". They are felt to be in balance, "correct", and in harmony with one another. Aesthetic values are important under extreme conditions. Perhaps this accounts for the famous colour master-plan of the winter city of Longyearbyen on Svalbard (78 degrees N of the equator) by Norwegian interior architect Grete Smedal. Since most of the buildings were owned and managed by a single company – Store Norske Spitsbergen Kullkompani A/S – it decided, in 1981, to commission a plan for the colouration of all its buildings and plant. The objective was to "enrich the environment, identify individual buildings and districts, and give the whole city a colour identity".

Greater attention to providing colour in the landscape, than has previously been accorded, will go a long way toward making urban space feel "warm", welcoming, and attractive. Landscape architect, Walter Kehm, of Canada stated that (Kehm, 1985, p. 59):

> my vision of the livable winter city includes simple and brave statements of environmental art, visually stimulating buildings, and streetscapes where colour, lighting, planting and wind protection elements are brought together in a meaningful way. Cosmetic "streetscaping" is not enough.

Although the improvements to everyday life can be significant through application of the above principles, there is still much to learn through research about climatically-sensitive design and site planning in northern regions. Much of the available literature to date has concentrated on hot, arid zones, usually in developing countries (Gut and Ackerknecht, 1993). This fact, alone, hinders policy analysts and urban designers working in winter climates.

The following approaches should be followed if climate-responsive and energy-efficient urban reorganization are to be achieved in the north. These are viewed from a perspective of urban design concepts, policy development, and regional planning strategies, and constitute the basis of design for a meaningful and humane urban habitat.

1. *Compact Urban Form*
Inhospitable surroundings should be 'walled-out' by clustering buildings and using vegetation, windscreens, snow fences, shelterbelts and a spatial configuration which is relatively compact. These techniques will assist in achieving a favourable micro-climate, and in substantial energy conservation.

2. *Orientation of Footpaths, Streets and Dwellings*
These should be designed so as to mitigate against adverse climatic forces impinging on the site and to maximize passive solar gain wherever possible.

3. *Enclosed Residential Courtyard Concept*
By arranging multi-family dwellings around interior courtyards, a more pleasant micro-climate is produced whereby wind turbulence and velocity can be significantly reduced. An improved potential for social networking is also made possible.

4. *Climatic Simulation Modelling*
During the initial design stages, wind tunnel testing and shadow pattern impacts (through application of the heliodon or similar computer techniques) are advised. This will help to establish fundamental relationships with respect to building bulk, shape, and location.

5. *Higher Densities*
In the residential, retail and commercial sectors, increasing densities can result in significant reductions to space heating requirements and will reduce transportation energy demand minimizing the need for spatial displacement.

6. *Multi-Use Buildings*
Buildings containing a diversity of uses or functions, e.g. shops, offices, residences, public facilities (cinemas, restaurants, post offices, schools), can potentially minimize the necessity for movement – especially under harsh conditions.

7. *Mixed Land Use*
Mixing land uses in neighbourhoods within the urban configuration – as opposed to segregation of uses through traditional zoning practices – will reduce the need for commuting. This creates greater self-sufficiency as a broad range of services can be made economically available with improved accessibility by private or public modes of transportation – which include walking and cycling. Mixed-use nodal development is an effective technique for tightening regional form.

8. *Intensification of Functions*
This implies more intensive use of existing land which is vacant and awaiting development (as well as redevelopment), including urban infill. Services and housing are the usual fabric at the neighbourhood level although commercial, retail, and even institutional uses can be incorporated, as can public transit installations. Where warranted by local market conditions, single-family houses can be converted to multiple-family use.

9. *Public Transit*
This is the most energy-efficient form of movement but to be cost-effective it must serve areas of relatively high density. There is strong compatibility between higher density, mixed use development and the provision of improved public transit serving transportation corridors and linking nodes of concentrated development.

Majorstuhöyden (architects R. Erskine & N. Torp) – project for Greater Oslo region (village centre).

All the elements of a Nordic design "grammar" are present. These incorporate mixed-use, arcades, well illuminated areas (using glass generously), solar access, micro-climatic space, pedestrian zones, and human scale.

Source: publicity brochure Aker Eiendom, Bergen Bank, Åke Larson construction.

10. *Total or Partial Climate-Protection*
In certain high-use areas, it is useful to connect buildings via galletias, arcades, canopied (or even glazed-in) sidewalks, and pedestrian networks leading to primary nodes of activity such as shopping, schools, cultural centres and transit stops (with well-designed, heated bus shelters). Simultaneously, creation of welcoming outdoor public space for use during the marginal seasons should be realized.

It is difficult to refute the fact that weather is among the most important forces influencing our lives. Insufficient attention has, thus far, been paid to this fact. Applied climatology can make a powerful impact in the various phases of the planning, building and design processes if taken seriously. It can assist in improving the quality of urban existence. Alternatively, disregard for such an approach may result in harmful and undesirable effects.

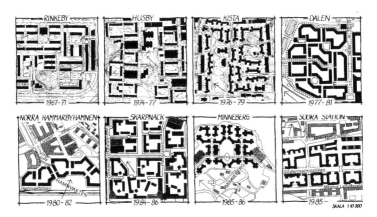

Courtyard Housing Estates, Greater Stockholm Region.
Source: Building Stockholm, op.cit., p.47.

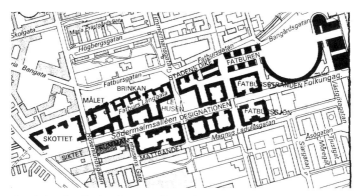

South Station Redevelopment Zone, Stockholm.
Source: Building Stockholm, Swedish Council for Building Research, Stockholm, 1986, p.70
(Project Leader: Per Kallstenius).

Project for the Helsinki Western Harbour.

Ecological courtyard blocks incorporate a multi-functional building texture with a hierarchy of private and semi-private open spaces.

Source: CASE architects & planners, Anne Børve, Eilif Bjørge & Kimmo Kuismanen.

Proposal for a covered walkway through the City of Alta, Norway incorporating pedestrians and cyclists.

Source: CASE architects & planners, Anne Brit Børve, Eilif Bjørge & Kimmo Kuismanen.

Proposed "stone-sculpture" for Alta, Norway.

The high stones protect people from the wind while reflecting heat, when south-facing.

Source: Anne Brit Børve (Oslo) and Eilif Bjørge (Bergen).

Proposed multi-purpose building designed by Ralph Erskine, in the North Harbour of Luleå, uses a configuration which maximizes solar access from the low sun angle at 66N latitude. The built form and roof contours employ aerodynamic shapes, reducing wind turbulence.

Source: Ralph Erskine, architect, Drottningholm.

View over town roofs
to the South Fjord.

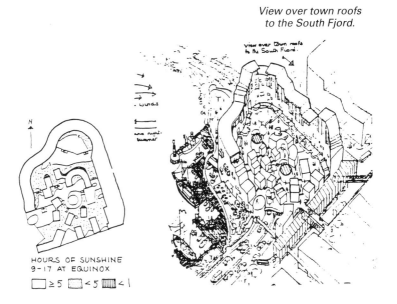

HOURS OF SUNSHINE
9-17 AT EQUINOX

□ ≥5 ▢ <5 ▥ <1

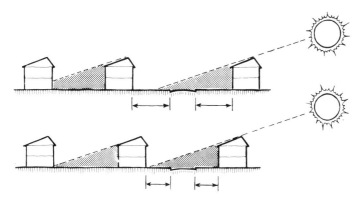

Section through typical residential street.
A reduction in front yard setbacks may improve solar access
opportunities – applying zoning by-laws.

Source: Land Use Planning for Energy Conservation,
Ontario Ministry of Municipal Affairs and Housing.

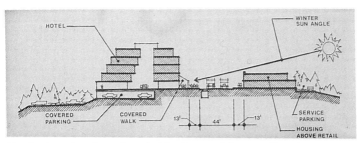

Idealized section through typical 'main street' for a northern town:
proposed new capital for Alaska.

Source: Sedway Cooke Associates, architects and planners, U.S.A.

ACHIEVING A SUSTAINABLE FUTURE

In an era in which the sustainable society has become a global imperative, and in which bio-diversity is more essential than it has ever been in the history of humankind, every effort shall have to be made to ensure that urban development is in complete harmony with each natural and human-made system. Perhaps the clearest articulation of this approach, which has a direct bearing on the built environment, was made by the International Union of Architects at its Chicago Congress (18-21 June 1993). In its "Declaration of Interdependence for a Sustainable Future", it emphatically recognized that (International Union of Architects, 1993, p. 1):

> We are ecologically interdependent with the whole natural environment; we are socially, culturally and economically interdependent with all of humanity; sustainability, in the context of this interdependence requires partnership, equity and balance among all parties;

> Buildings and the built environment play a major role in the human impact on the natural environment and on the quality of life; sustainable design integrates consideration of resource and energy efficiency, healthy buildings and materials, ecologically and socially sensitive land-use and an aesthetic sensitivity that inspires, affirms and ennobles; sustainable design can significantly reduce adverse human impacts on the natural environment while simultaneously improving quality of life and economic well-being.

In such a context, a commitment was made to "place environmental and social sustainability at the core" of its practices and professional responsibilities; to develop and improve procedures, practices, products, services and standards that would enable the implementation of sustainable design – while bringing existing and future elements of the built environment, in their design, production, use, and eventual reuse, up to sustainable design standards.

Within a framework of designing, planning and building northern habitats, the harsher the prevailing local conditions, the more cautious one must be – in the long term – if we are to achieve a *sustainable* future. Highly precise and detailed consideration of climatological, social, economic, cultural and ecological parameters will have to be integrated within planning policy, programs and practices. If we are to move toward a framework of sustainable development, the following points must be seriously considered[2]:

1. Land is under quantitative threat and qualitative abuse from economic activity, tourism, capital investment and other sources. It must, therefore, be protected carefully, for it is a non-renewable resource. It is a vital element in determining human activity. Assessing risks and assigning priorities for its utilization are of the utmost importance.

2. There will always be conflicts between the desire to develop the north and the need to preserve its fragile ecosystems. A healthy balance must be achieved among these goals.

3. In an atmosphere of looser regulations and stronger private initiative, people must have access to better information about planning and design issues so that they understand the hazards and risks and the long-range

impacts of present-day decisions concerning such important matters as energy, waste, air and water quality, transportation and dwelling.

4. Innovative ideas – which frequently emerge from grass-roots organizations – must be supported, and promoted by local government if implementation is to be realized. Further monitoring and evaluation on a follow-up basis will be extremely helpful in assessing the validity of the innovations and their degree of applicability to other situations in different regions.

5. Economic growth, high living standards and expectations have, over time, ruined our atmosphere, disrupted the traditional life-style patterns (e.g. Aboriginal Peoples), and destroyed local values and architectural heritage. Often, this has been hastened through large-scale, centralized decision-making. Therefore, alternative approaches have to be sought which are multi-functional in essence, more self-contained in terms of production, consumption, recycling capacity (e.g. sewage, water, waste, energy, etc.) and which behave in an environmentally responsible manner.

6. Creative energies must urgently be harnessed and mobilized in order to realize the best available solutions to challenges in a variety of cultural and climatic contexts. Present-day 'high-technology' will have to be fused with traditional knowledge and vernacular 'low-technology' principles and practice using ecological concepts if environmentally-sensitive results are ultimately to appear.

7. Regional identity in architectural and urbanistic expression (colour, form, texture, materials, etc.) should be encouraged as an essential goal. Standardization of building techniques and methods throughout Europe and

North America has resulted in stylistic uniformity and a 'neutralization' of built form. This should be avoided wherever possible.

8. The concept of sustainable development will have to be institutionalized within practices in both the public and private sectors. This may mean a dramatic shift in attitudes, values and even legislative frameworks which reward and penalize activities through equitable incentive and disincentive systems.

9. A *sustainable* ethic must be the only basis for future development: ... one which meets contemporary needs without destroying, hindering, disrupting or endangering possibilities of a high quality existence for future generations.

Putting these ideas into practice means that both rationalizing and perhaps even limiting energy production and consumption may have to occur. The scatterization and urban sprawl which has been the pattern of metropolitan urbanization may have to be contained, through policies which de-emphasize the car and place attention on more efficient public transport – and gentler, cleaner motorized traffic – applying a broad variety of traffic-calming techniques (Zuckermann, 1991) which are now commonplace throughout most Western European cities. There are severe consequences of a continued growth, or even a stabilization of motor-car use. These are air pollution (causing danger to public health), the proliferation of acid rain, destruction of the ozone layer, noise, hazard, high energy consumption, and further fragmentation of the urban tissue. Conservation of natural resources must become the norm, together with a way of building which is highly respectful of nature.

The Finnish Government, through its National Environment Policy Plan concluded that (Rautsi, 1992, p. 159):

> some of the effects of the sustainable development principle for the Finnish built environment (are) that national level physical planning will be included in the system; sparse settlements in the countryside will be brought under planning; irrational spreading of shopping along motorways will be prevented; measures to improve the environmental quality of urban centres will be created.

Canadian responses will likely be predicated on many of the same variables which would influence Finnish practices, given the similarity in national settlement structure and of climate in both countries. Comparative studies – and international cooperation – of sustainable development design guidelines will go a long way toward achieving substantial progress in a variety of northern habitat conditions.

WINTER LIVING: OPTIONS AND STRATEGIES

Prior to being capable of generating action strategies, acceptable sets of goals and policies will have to be developed. These shall have to be viewed within both short and long terms. As such, they will be subjected to one of the major dilemmas in urban planning and policy-making – balancing the sectoral versus the comprehensive approaches amongst which there exists a constant tension. Furthermore, there is a complementary tension operative within this larger frame – that of the individual's needs versus those of society.

What can northern settlements do if they wish to make their environments more convenient, efficient, attractive and comfortable during the winter season? At once, it becomes clear that if comprehensive solutions are desired, they must encompass the entire field of settlement patterns including the social, political, cultural and economic structures of communities. Four scales of intervention will have to be addressed:

1. *The regional level:* which has the overall settlement pattern, and movement systems, as focal elements.

2. *The city structure/macro-level:* which has the total territory of a city as its field of attention. Here, one is concerned with distribution of uses and activities as well as with provision of services and transportation facilities.

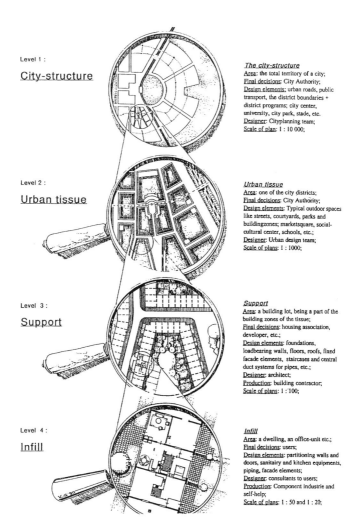

Level 1 :

City-structure

The city-structure
Area: the total territory of a city;
Final decisions: City Authority;
Design elements: urban roads, public
transport, the district boundaries +
district programs; city center,
university, city park, stade, etc.
Designer: Cityplanning team;
Scale of plan: 1 : 10 000;

Level 2 :

Urban tissue

Urban tissue
Area: one of the city districts;
Final decisions: City Authority;
Design elements: Typical outdoor spaces
like streets, courtyards, parks and
buildingzones; marketsquare, social-
cultural center, schools, etc.;
Designer: Urban design team;
Scale of plans: 1 : 1000;

Level 3 :

Support

Support
Area: a building lot, being a part of the
building zones of the tissue;
Final decisions: housing association,
developer, etc.;
Design elements: foundations,
loadbearing walls, floors, roofs, fixed
facade elements, staircases and central
duct systems for pipes, etc.;
Designer: architect;
Production: building contractor;
Scale of plans: 1 :'100;

Level 4 :

Infill

Infill
Area: a dwelling, an office-unit etc.;
Final decisions: users;
Design elements: partitioning walls and
doors, sanitairy and kitchen equipments,
piping, facade elements;
Designer: consultants to users;
Production: Component industrie and
self-help;
Scale of plans: 1 : 50 and 1 : 20;

The Different Levels of Intervention.
Source: Frans van der Werf, The European City Today.
Helsinki, Ministry of the Environment, 1993.

3. *The urban tissue/neighbourhood level:* which has the urban tissue of the districts or neighbourhoods as the field of concern. Issues such as building types and orientation, land use, site planning, parks, squares, local climate, floor area ratios, building bulk, development profiles, and urban design are critical.

4. *The support/building level:* which is concerned with the specific building lot (part of the components of the urban tissue), internal design and layout, materials, and technical installations.

Complementing the city's spatial structure, four categories of critical issues which require attention and must be addressed are :

Physical issues: pedestrian protection, accessibility optimization, integrated development, public open space, and snow removal.

Social issues: safety and health care, winter promotion events, projecting positive images of winter, community participation, and planning for special needs groups.

Economic issues: transit assistance, winter subsidy programs, tourism promotion, employment and job retraining.

Policy issues: In addition to the more detailed measures, there are numerous strategies which can make an impact when approaching the meso-scale (street, urban block, neighbourhood, precinct) and macro-scale (district, town, metropolitan area). This orientation could be designated "winter management", "seasonal development", and "educational programs".

Human behaviour characteristics under cold conditions have powerful implications with respect to the performance of bureaucratic structures, law enforcement agencies, public behaviour which may or may not be tolerated, and similarly related institutional norms. *Winter utilization of cities might benefit from different approaches to policy formulation than summer usage of the same cities and their facilities.* Responses to such questions – including time management – have not been made entirely clear yet, and serve as excellent areas for further investigation.

Since most efforts, to date, have been directed toward the individual building level, the macro-level, regional, and neighbourhood scales will have to receive increased attention. The livable winter city will have to deal with a broad spectrum of issues. The highest priority ones, amongst others, should include the following (Pressman and Zepic, 1986, pp. 125-126):

1. *Think Winter*
A radical readjustment will have to occur regarding our ingrained habit of thinking negatively about winter. More ways of inducing positive images will have to evolve, e.g. attitude modification through education. Professionals will have to direct greater emphasis in design and management toward the winter and marginal seasons.

2. *Do More With What We Have*
Solutions will have to be energy-efficient, cost-effective and climate-sensitive. More effective ways to reuse and retrofit existing spaces and facilities will have to be developed. Revised policies and regulatory instruments may have to be put in place to improve incrementally what already exists. Innovative approaches must be encouraged through techniques such as design competitions.

3. *Attitudes and Lifestyles*

Reallocation of time should be studied to more effectively utilize shorter daylight hours during mid-winter (especially at high latitudes). We must take advantage of the dramatic seasonal contrasts and even consider recreation (cross-country skiing or ice skating) as a mode of travel. Skid-control driving techniques should be made mandatory – as they have been for a long time, in a number of Nordic nations.

4. *Improving the Urban Infrastructure*

Winter-oriented management of the infrastructure is urgently required. Public transit should be comfortable, convenient and accessible (through heated bus shelters and reduced headways between buses during the coldest parts of winter). Micro-climatic spaces must be developed together with enclosed and semi-enclosed public space, linking essential movements, e.g. parking garages, transit stations, institutional functions, etc.

5. *Exterior Public Space should be Winter-Friendly*

Cities require more fountains, water, trees, and pleasant places for sitting (protected from wind and exposed to sun), chatting, daydreaming, relaxing – embodying high standards of aesthetic quality in the urban furnishings and landscape features. Especially in chilly climates, the presence of sunlight and absence of wind are significant factors in explaining why some public spaces attract people and why others repel them.

6. *Architecture and Design*

Matters of colour, form, texture, shape and volume must be more in keeping with the spirit of winter and its appreciation. Multiple-use spaces will have to be provided within a framework that interrelates indoors and outdoors.

7. *Visual Environment*
Four-season open spaces – incorporating winter gardens – which include colourful features such as flags, banners, sculpture, fountains that delight in all seasons, and civic art forms, should help to enhance and animate the northern context and use it as a source of inspiration. Clues should be taken from nature and its dramatic transformations with the changing seasons.

8. *Inject the City with Lively Centres*
The city must be imbued with constructive energy which promotes civic life, ease in shopping, business, and movement on foot, and which offers a high level of sensory stimulation, delight and variety – while reducing stress caused by cold temperatures. It needs lively, informal meeting places both indoors and out-of-doors.

9. *Stimulate Neighbourhood Action/Civic Activity*
Carnivals, winter festivals, and celebrations should promote positive winter images throughout various neighbourhoods, within the central business district, and throughout the entire metropolitan area.

10. *More Research is Imperative*
Post-occupancy evaluation of public urban spaces, user analysis, participant observation with interview and questionnaire techniques will be required if we are to discover which elements of winter are appreciated by urban dwellers and which are viewed as nuisances.

There can be little doubt that our urban environments must serve not only as places for making a living but also as sources of inspiration – where the "meaning of life" becomes at least as important as the "means to life". If we are truly concerned with making cities more habitable, our interventions shall have to work toward the creation of improved aesthetics both in built and unbuilt space, improvements in social and economic opportunities, and toward the genuine acceptance of management and organizational strategies which are responsive to the goal of accommodating human needs within the constraints of climatic demands.

Further Action and Research

From existing applied research and policy development experiences, conducted both in Europe and North America, in almost every community one can find instances of ideas, policies, programs, and projects which address issues of energy conservation and climatically-responsible planning and design. However, these responses are often fragmented and normally deal with only one, or sometimes several aspects of the problem. In a majority of cases, solutions are focussed on one issue at a time, for this tends to be simpler from an administrative point of view concerning implementation. Treatment of a multi-faceted problem, from a holistic perspective, is much more complicated and this would seem to be the reason for fragmented approaches.

Planning decisions and their implementation within the urban field normally fall under the jurisdiction of multiple agencies, authorities and departments (e.g. parks & recreation, transportation, housing, roads, sewage, water supply, social services, etc.), each of which is charged with specific responsibilities and is answerable to elected officials, on the one hand, and to the public, on the other hand. The task of coordination in all these sectors makes effective management difficult to achieve.

Urban planning has frequently been both restrictive and reactive in its nature and orientation, particularly in North

America. It has been conservative in its outlook and has primarily played an advisory role. Generally speaking, it is concerned with choices and policy options – where certain groups will benefit at the expense of others. Planning has usually focussed on the preservation of the status quo rather than on the testing of future possibilities which tend to increase choice and to open up new directions for community creativity in social, economic and physical realms. Any approach more radical than the one we have witnessed would be tantamount to questioning the fundamental principles and practices upon which planning has been predicated for the past half century.

Insofar as environments can be considered – indeed, must be considered – to be complete, spatially integrated entities, effective "winter planning" policies can only be achieved if these are, conceptually and practically, made an integral component of the comprehensive planning, development, and design processes. Applications of climate-responsive principles will have to be simultaneously applied to the micro-, meso-, and macro-scales of the urban pattern if cities in northern regions are to be reshaped and reorganized humanely. Coordination among all the disciplines involved in ameliorating urban life under harsh conditions will be absolutely essential. Boundaries which have traditionally isolated disciplines, e.g. architectural and industrial design, landscape architecture, applied climatology, social policy development, and urban planning, will have to be removed with increasing information exchange occurring if real progress is to result.

Design and policy decisions should be related to the behavioural sciences – particularly environmental sociology, anthropology, and psychology. Nourishment received from these sources can make noteworthy strides toward improving winter living. Through interdisciplinary collaboration, planners, designers and policy analysts have the possibility of becoming more socially responsible. Reciprocally, behavioural experts will have greater opportunities in the realm of applying their findings in more practical ways. With such joint activity, those working in the gap between social needs and design responses – dealing with the interactions of people, society and the built environment – can more meaningfully contribute to developing the knowledge base affecting these concerns.

In order to advance knowledge and actions in the face of severe climate, we must understand how to harness the decisive forces behind most private and public decision-making in all sectors of urban and regional development. Problems will have to be viewed within a context which integrates management and planning of existing urban systems from the spatial and temporal angles. Last but not least, the quality of urban living will have to be improved continuously, community and individual consciousness must be increased, and urban dwellers will have to be well informed so that they may participate meaningfully in collective decisions.

Although considerable information can now readily be accessed (civilization has existed in northern areas for thousands of years and is tradition-rich), much of the work in the field of "winter livability" is still in the stage of infancy and shall continue to evolve. There is a need for further research concerning the application of winter habitability concepts to particular climatic circumstances. All the actors directly or indirectly involved in the building, planning and development industries will have to become experts in understanding which elements contribute, in the most useful ways, to easing winter-induced discomfort and to enhancing the positive benefits and joys of the winter season.

Future research should assist in resolving the dilemmas inherent in the "winter cities" problematic. In addition to answering questions of a more theoretical nature regarding the effect of climate on behaviour, research should also contribute to the development of social and physical planning guidelines and interventions including both spatial and aspatial elements dealing with human well-being.

We shall have to think and act very courageously. Innovative policies will have to be monitored in terms of cost-effectiveness and user satisfaction. They will have to extend to a wide level of spheres dealing with life in cold climates – not only housing form, land use and transportation, but also clothing, home maintenance, community welfare, family and friendship networks, leisure activities and time management.

The choices we make will ultimately determine what kinds of environments we shall have. The debate on what is "desirable" will have to broaden its base. Urban policies will have to reinforce these "desired" development patterns. We shall all have to ponder what types of cities and communities we want – and for what kind of a society. Policies will have to be harnessed so that the likelihood of attaining our goals will be based on realistic expectations putting them within reach of the available means.

New York – Rockefeller Center Skating Rink in downtown Manhattan possesses a powerful sense of place.

Photo: N. Pressman.

Don Valley, Toronto.
Cross-country skiing is possible right in the heart of Toronto, protected from noise and traffic.

Photo: N. Pressman.

CONCLUSIONS

Priorities for Built Form

It is acknowledged that only the sensitive integration of skills from the disciplines of architecture, landscape design, applied engineering, and urban planning will be capable of improving comfort within a frequently disorganized urban fabric. If winter problems are to be reduced, it will be essential:

– to *integrate* concepts and techniques from the above fields in order to better control human comfort;

– to *relate* goals for obtaining physically improved comfort to cultural, biophysical and economic conditions in order to ascertain the extent to which application is feasible within planning practice;

– to *target* objectives which are based on specific problem areas in the full recognition that multi-disciplinary approaches and co- operation may be essential if the most useful results are to be anticipated.

Only a *cumulative* effect of various strategies and actions can produce dramatic results. There is the constant danger of interpretation regarding the relative importance of the techniques which can alleviate winter-induced discomfort. All strategies are inherently related. Which are most applicable to specific situations will often depend on socio-cultural factors (e.g. priorities perceived by certain user groups). Therefore, it will be essential to determine criteria which are overriding for each individual setting, applying those techniques which seem most compatible with the local issues. In order to obtain immediate reduction of winter discomfort, *incremental* and *short-term* solutions at relatively low costs, will be necessary. Through a demonstration that even seemingly small transformations to the physical milieu can ease many difficulties associated with the cold, dark season, it will be easier to gain the public and political support required to achieve more elaborate long-term goals.

The variables which can be manipulated significantly affect both public and private interests. They mostly address the following key issues (Pressman, 1988 a):

1. *Land-use Policy*
   - emphasis on compact urban form and reduction of sprawl.
   - changes to conventional practices on land parcels (e.g. more mixed use).
   - variations to street widths and reduction or elimination of "segregated use" zoning.
   - appropriate street layout, orientation, and siting of buildings with proper provision for snow deposit areas.

2. *Transportation*
   - changes to existing curb details (sidewalk/roadway interface).
   - improved maintenance procedures and selective use of sheltering devices.
   - transit scheduling based on "seasonal demand".
   - shift away from cars to "greener" modes (car-pooling, transit, cycling, electric cars, walking – and even skiing).

3. *Massing and Building Controls*
   - desirability of wind impact and snow drifting statements.
   - shadowing studies for new development and redevelopment.
   - solar access rights guaranteed under normal conditions.
   - innovative climate-responsive built form encouraged through competitions.

4. *Open Space/Outdoor Living Areas*
   - application of micro-climatic principles to improve thermal comfort.
   - vegetation selected for improved aesthetic quality and comfort for walking, sitting and playing.
   - snow fences to control drifting.
   - windbreaks and shelterbelts to provide protection by reducing wind velocity.

5. *Public Amenities*
   - sensitively designed public seating areas and meeting places (using appropriate materials).
   - bus shelters provided at intensively used nodes serving high-quality residential and city centre areas (heated at strategic, high-use locations).
   - canopies, gallerias, colonnades, arcades for pedestrian protection where acting as connecting links between important parts of a site or between different sites (this can include "skywalks" and underground connections).
   - increase sensory stimulation and animate public spaces, ensuring safety through effective illumination.

What is important is the recognition that explicit winter-induced discomforts exist and that they be acknowledged in planning practice. Once this occurs, our city centres and residential precincts can function satisfactorily.

Adopting a Climate-Sensitive Approach

Achieving suitable micro-climatic conditions will undoubtedly enhance the quality of urban life. Therefore, performance standards which protect pedestrians and cyclists from increased wind speeds induced by design and positioning of buildings must be formulated. These should be combined with measures to guarantee daylighting requirements, proper air circulation and sunlight access – through regulating built form, using front and rear sky exposure planes – especially in areas of intense public use (City of Toronto, 1990, pp. 42-44).

The environments benefiting from climate-protection strategies and improved micro-climatic conditions should be those which connect important nodes of activity such as shops and public transport stops, public squares and cycle-parking zones, major institutional buildings and high-use functions (e.g. railway or bus stations). If these strategies also contribute toward energy conservation and environmental protection, they will have made a powerful impact in improving urban quality. Both physical design and social organization have to work together to support everyday life, and urban architecture has an important role to play. Urban design concept plans should indicate major pedestrian links between origins and destinations suggesting where climatically sheltered zones might be realized.

In deciding on the levels of priority for weather-protection, the needs of various user groups must be carefully specified. User characteristics vis-à-vis trips (origins and destinations) will determine the dominant movement networks, their specific locations and the detailing of the sheltering elements, within the overall framework of the town or district. The extent of protection will have to be seen as a function of both need and cost. *In areas of signifi-*

cant pedestrian and cycle activity, consideration should be given to requiring weather protection devices such as canopies, awnings, arcades, and colonnades.

Attractive and well managed streets and open spaces – and the planned and spontaneous activities which occur in them – form the essence of urban life. They should be genuinely public in nature as a counterthrust to the gradual erosion of the public domain resulting from large "atrium-style" pseudo-public environments and shopping malls located downtown and in the suburbs. Once out of either the car or public transportation, *everyone eventually becomes a pedestrian.* Therefore, it is essential to direct greater attention to the achievement of a milieu in which the slow-mode is dominant (Bach/Pressman, 1992, p. 91).

It will be important to extend the outdoor season (in colder regions) encouraging people to remain outdoors at times when they might normally withdraw indoors. Climatic modification of the environment is required if human animation is to thrive in our urban centres during the colder periods. Even if outdoor social space and the activities which it harbours suffer a reduction during the cold part of the year, social activity can still be supported and maintained.

If improved bioclimatic conditions and more humane urban environments are to be achieved, the following will have to receive high priority:

1. Careful decisions must be taken regarding the types and location of vegetation and planting for modifying climatic conditions.

2. Multiple use of public space over varying times of the day (or night), week or even year, will ensure greater activity and animation adding to the perceived importance of the space as well as to user safety and satisfaction.

3. High-quality shelter, especially at public transport stops and high-intensity cycle use areas, is desirable.

4. Alternative micro-climates should optimally be possible in the same space (some areas in shade, others exposed to sun – with varying degrees of protection from wind). Flexible use of space will result.

5. Comfort criteria should be established for all seasons, where possible (especially if considerable seasonal variation occurs).

6. The attempt to minimize both travel time and distance for cycle users and pedestrians constitutes the most important principle if reduction of motor car traffic is desired. The concepts of short-cutting and climatic protection can serve either as determining or modifying factors vis-à-vis movement patterns within the urban fabric.

Flexible utilization of the public realm, in different seasons, will ensure improved livability for users regardless of their needs or trip destinations. Adopting a climate-sensitive approach (in less than ideal climatic regions) is clearly the best strategy (when combined with appropriate, user-responsive, ergonomic design) for obtaining a 'sustainable' lifestyle well into the foreseeable future.

> Managing of a large scale 'climatic environment' where the sub-components are town and region, involves accommodation to the rhythm of annual seasons. This begins to determine the character of the urban design and structure of the land-use. The criterion for a livable town is its potential to respond to weather agents during different seasons of the year (Pietilä, 1988).

Future Directions

There is clearly a considerable amount of existing climatological knowledge which has the potential of being applied
to architecture, urban design, and town and regional planning. However, such information is not always available in a
form that can be easily used, or applied, by architects,
designers or urban planners. Hence, there is a need to translate it into directly usable design criteria, building standards,
norms, principles and urban design guidelines for application by the above professionals – which also includes engineers, policy analysts, landscape architects and other related
disciplines. New "cold-climate" design standards – and
solutions – will be essential and can ultimately be expected
to emerge.

Planners, designers and policy-makers must encourage
and promote application of climatological know-how in land
use and urban design concepts, while keeping abreast of
newly developing information. Builders should be provided
incentives to demonstrate advantages of climate-adapted
projects on particular sites. Local governments must embrace
climatically-sensitive development as part of their policies
through the adoption of new design guidelines, revision of
master plans and zoning by-laws, and inclusion of climate-
oriented performance standards in competition programs.
Finally, approval for building and site planning projects
should be subjected to rigorous review of how well designs
are adapted to the local conditions in conformity with
explicitly-stated "winter livability" structure plans.

The physical environment of the winter city can either
support or impede the formation of social activities in outdoor public space. Social activities are particularly important for mental health in winter due to isolation and other
multiple stresses that impact on people during the cold,

often inhospitable season. Life in urban public space can be encouraged by also providing a high quality aesthetic environment. Urban space should be designed using microclimatic principles that block winter winds and allow sunlight to penetrate between buildings. Application of these principles can extend the summer and marginal seasons and even allow summer-type activities (e.g. sitting in the sun) to take place on mild winter days. Based on Norwegian studies, architects Ralph Erskine and Boris Culjat from Sweden have suggested that the outdoor season could be extended by up to six weeks by simply using micro-climatic planning and design principles (Culjat and Erskine, 1988, p. 353).

These studies have demonstrated that in the late autumn, people usually cease using outdoor space at 11 degrees Celsius. In the spring, they return again to the outdoors at roughly 9 degrees Celsius, as their bodies have acclimatized to lower temperatures and they have an urge to be outdoors after their winter confinement.

While not all "summer" activities must be abandoned during the winter, especially where these are of an outdoor-type, micro-climatic control of the environment is, nevertheless, essential if some human animation and life is to be retained outside. The main principles which are to be incorporated should be year-round *useability, contact with nature, user participation, and cultural continuity* – implying that the chosen shapes, volumes, textures, colours, materials and urban spaces between buildings should reflect the landscape and cultural heritage of the environs.

Innovatively organized housing and urban development competitions can assist in demonstrating – through pilot projects – precisely how physical interventions can improve the quality of life in northern environments. Practical lessons emerging from such competitions and other landmark project designs will point to desirable ways of creating climatically-adapted designs and plans. Research and discussion, with follow-up monitoring and evaluation, are crucial.

There has always been broad agreement that the built environment – composed of cultivated nature, buildings, open space systems, towns and regions, and the natural landscape – is a most precious, common resource that cannot be managed carelessly. The long-term sustainability of water, land and air is essential. Designing and building according to a climate-sensitive approach can be one additional way in which we can all be environmentally responsible, and in which, under the proper conditions, we can transform *'space'* into *'place'* while preserving the biodiversity needed to support life on planet earth.

Finally, as design will continue to play an ever-increasing role in the 21st century, it will be absolutely necessary to strike an optimum balance between preserving nature and shaping a high-quality built environment. We urgently need, today, to create the trends which, in future, will offer the environments we deserve. They must ensure that all people experience ideal conditions of human well-being, habitation, work, and intellectual development in each of the four seasons.

NOTES

1 Five recent examples of this newly emerging literature are *Cities Designed for Winter,* Jorma Mänty and Norman Pressman, editors (Building Book Ltd., Helsinki), 1988; *Design for Northern Climates,* Vladimir Matus (Van Nostrand Reinhold), 1988; *Habitat International, Vol. 13, No. 2* (Pergamon Press), 1989 – theme issue on "Settlements in Harsh Living Conditions", Jussi Rautsi, Norman Pressman, Tom Davies, guest editors (Proceedings of the Turku 1988 UN/ECE Research Colloquium); *Neighbourhood Planning and Housing Design in Cold and Subarctic Areas,* Ministry of the Environment – Norway, October 1992 (Proceedings of the ECE Colloquium, Tromsø, Norway 1990); *Climate-Sensitive Urban Space,* Boudewijn Bach and Norman Pressman (Faculteit der Bouwkunde, Delft University of Technology), 1992.

2 Based on the U.N. Economic Commission for Europe Research Colloquium on *Neighbourhood Planning and Housing Design in Cold and Subarctic Areas,* October 1992, Oslo, Norway (Norman Pressman – chief rapporteur).

REFERENCES

Altman, I. and M.M. Chemers. *Culture and Environment.* Monterey, California: Brooks/Cole Publishing Co., 1980.

Anderes, F. and A. Agranoff. *Ice Palaces.* Toronto, Canada: Macmillan of Canada, 1983.

Andersen, P.A., Lustig, M.W. and J.F. Andersen. "Changes in Latitude, Changes in Attitude: The Relationship Between Climate and Interpersonal Communication Predispositions". *Communication Quarterly,* Vol. 38, No. 4, Fall 1990.

Architectural Design, 11/12, (special issue on "The Architecture of Ralph Erskine"), U.K. 1977.

Bach, B. and N. Pressman. *Climate-Sensitive Urban Space.* Delft: Publicatieburo, Faculteit der Bouwkunde, Technische Universiteit Delft (The Netherlands), 1992.

Beckman, R.M. and D. Ackerknecht. "Growth as Tradition: Bern, A Traditional Settlement in Change". *Traditional Dwellings and Settlements Review,* Vol. V, No. 1, Fall 1993.

Bertheussen, K. "Experiences with the Use of Design Criteria (Norway)". *Neighbourhood Planning and Housing Design in Cold and Subarctic Areas.* Oslo, Norway: Ministry of Environment, October 1992.

Blumenfeld, H. "Problems of Winter in the City". *Reshaping Winter Cities.* Norman Pressman (Ed), Waterloo: University of Waterloo Press/Livable Winter City Association, 1985.

Boyles, P. "New Light on Winter Darkness". *Yankee*. February, 1988.

The Business of Winter (The Economist Publications Limited, London, England), commissioned and published by the Winter Cities Conference Corporation, Edmonton, Alberta, Canada, 1988.

Byggekunst, The Norwegian Review of Architecture – special issue on "Nordiske Tendenser" (Nordic Tendencies), Vol. 7, Oslo: 1986.

Caborn, J.M. *Shelterbelts and Windbreaks*. London: Faber and Faber, 1965.

Canada Mortgage and Housing Corporation. *Outdoor Living Areas Advisory Document*. Ottawa, Canada, 1981.

The Canadian Encyclopedia. Edmonton: Hurtig Publishers, 1985.

Cavell, E. and D. Reid. *When Winter Was King*. Banff: Altitude Publishing (in association with The Whyte Museum of the Canadian Rockies), 1988.

City of Toronto. *Cityplan '91 – Living Downtown in Toronto*. Toronto, Canada: (Consultant's Report, Vol. 1), 1988.

Condon, R.G. *Inuit Behavior and Seasonal Change in the Canadian Arctic*. UMI Research Press, 1983.

Collymore, P. *The Architecture of Ralph Erskine*. Great Britain: Granada Publishing, 1982.

Culjat, B. and R. Erskine. "Climate-Responsive Social Space: A Scandinavian Perspective". *Cities Designed for Winter* (Eds., Jorma Mänty & Norman Pressman) Helsinki: Building Book Ltd., 1988.

Day, C. *Places of the Soul.* Wellingborough, Northamptonshire, England: The Aquarian Press (Thorsons Publishing Group), 1990.

Dunin-Woyseth, H. "*Genius loci:* planning and the winter dimension". *Town Planning Review,* Vol. 61, No. 3. Liverpool: Liverpool University Press, July 1990.

ECE (Economic Commission for Europe) – *Research Colloquium on Livability of Human Settlements in Winter Climates.* Edmonton, Alberta, Canada: Committee on Housing, Building and Planning, Working Party on Urban & Regional Planning, Group of Experts on Urban & Regional Research, February 15-19, 1986.

Egli, E. *Climate and Town Districts – Consequences and Demands/Die Neue Stadt in Landschaft und Klima.* Erlenbach-Zürich: Verlag für Architektur AG, 1951.

Gehl, J. "A Changing Street Life in a Changing Society". *Places,* Vol. 6, No. 1 (fall), 1989.

Glaumann, M. *Design for Cold Climate.* Stockholm: Cold Climate Group Research Colloquium, (unpublished presentation paper), Royal Institute of Technology (KTH), 1990.

Gut, P. and D. Ackerknecht. *Climate Responsive Building: Appropriate Building Construction in Tropical and Subtropical Regions.* St. Gallen, Switzerland: SKAT (Swiss Centre for Development Cooperation in Technology and Management), 1993.

Hamelin, L.E. "Seeing the North with New Eyes" (by Lise Bissonnette). Toronto, Canada: *The Globe and Mail.* Saturday, April 23, 1988.

Hanen, H. and G. Liburd."Cold-Climate Neo-traditionalism" *Winter Cities,* Vol. 10, No. 4, March 1993.

Heine, C. "A Concept of Nordic Society With A Focus on the Canadian Arctic and the Development and Maintenance of Nordic Community Identity". Manuscript (acquired through personal correspondence), Inuvik, Northwest Territories, Canada, October 16, 1985.

Heschong, L. *Thermal Delight in Architecture.* Cambridge and London: MIT Press, 1985.

Hurlich, M.G. Environmental Adaptation: biological and behavioural response to cold in the Canadian Subarctic. *Ph.D. Dissertation.*, State University of New York at Buffalo. Unpublished, 1976.

Indian and Northern Affairs and External Affairs. *Circumpolar Community.* Ottawa, Canada: Information Canada, Ottawa, 1975.

International Union of Architects/Union Internationale des Architectes. *Newsletter,* June/July (English Edition). Paris, France, 1993.

Kehm, W. "The Landscape of the Livable Winter City", *Reshaping Winter Cities.* Norman Pressman, editor. Waterloo, Ontario, Canada: University of Waterloo Press & Livable Winter City Association,1985.

Knowles, R. *Sun, Rhythm, Form.* Cambridge, Massachusetts: MIT Press, 1981.

Krantz, B. "Everyday Life and Urban Habitat". Unpublished paper presented at the Winter Cities Workshop – Architecture and Territory – *North Calotte Architects Symposium.* Tromsø, Norway: June 17-19, 1988.

Krier, L. "The Reconstruction of the European City: An Outline for a Charter". *UIA International Architect,* Issue 7, 1985.

Lehrman, J. "The Skyway Assessed". *Making Cities Livable Newsletter*, Vol. 1, No. 4. December 1988.

Magnusson, S. *Northern Sphinx*. Reykjavik, Iceland: Snaebjorn Jonsson and Co., 1984.

Manker, E. *People of the Eight Seasons*. Gothenburg, Sweden: Tre Trykere, 1963.

Mänty, J. *Cities and Snow: Reflections from Finland*, manuscript, 1985 (acquired through personal correspondence).

Matus, V. *Design for Northern Climates*. New York: Van Nostrand Reinhold, 1988.

McIlroy, T. *The Winter Book*. Markham, Ontario: Arcadia House Inc., Saunders of Toronto Limited, 1985.

Municipality of Stockholm. *Kista, Husby, Akalla: A digest for Planners, Politicians and Critics*. Stockholm: 1983.

Nasgaard, R. *The Mystic North*. Toronto: University of Toronto Press, 1984.

Nash, J. "Relations in Frozen Places", unpublished paper presented at the Workshop *Curing the Common Cold*, Toronto, Ontario: February 21-22, 1986.

Norberg-Schulz, C. *Genius Loci*. New York: Rizzoli International Publications Inc.,1980.

Pekkanen, T. *Toivo Pekkanen's Thoughts*, (selected from his works by Antero Pekkanen), Porvoo, Finland: WSOY, 1962.

Persinger, M.A. *The Weather Matrix and Human Behaviour*. New York: Praeger, 1980.

Philips, D. "Planning with Winter Climate in Mind", *Cities Designed for Winter*, (J. Mänty & N. Pressman, eds.), Helsinki: Building Book Ltd., 1988.

Pietilä, R. "On Climate and Place" (Foreword). *Cities Designed for Winter* (eds., J. Mänty and N. Pressman) Helsinki: Building Book Ltd., 1988.

Pihlak, M. *Philosophy, Principles and Practice of Northern Latitude Urban Landscape Design.* M.L.A. Thesis, University of California at Berkeley. July 1983.

Pressman, N. *Sustainable Winter Cities: A Global Perspective.* Invited Paper presented at the Conference "Städer om Vintern" (Cities in Winter). Falun, Sweden. March 1, 1993.

Pressman, N. "Cultural Interpretations of The North". *Neighbourhood Planning and Housing Design in Cold and Subarctic Areas,* (Proceedings of the ECE Colloquium, Tromsø, Norway), Oslo, Norway: Ministry of Environment, October 1992.

Pressman, N. *Innovative Prototypes for Cold-Climate Neighbourhoods.* SSHRCC (Social Sciences and Humanities Research Council of Canada) Research Paper (unpublished), 1991.

Pressman, N. "Human Health and Social Factors in Winter Climates". *Energy and Buildings.* Vols. 15-16. The Netherlands: Elsevier Sequoia, 1990/91.

Pressman, N. *The Reduction of Winter-Induced Discomfort in Canadian Residential Areas.* Ottawa: Canada Mortgage and Housing Corporation, 1988 a.

Pressman, N. *Images of the North: Cultural Interpretations of Winter.* Winnipeg, Manitoba: Institute of Urban Studies, University of Winnipeg (Winter Communities Series No. 5), 1988 b.

Pressman, N. "The Survival of Winter Cities: Problems and Prospects". *The Future of Winter Cities* (G. Gappert, ed.). Urban Affairs Annual Reviews, Vol. 31. Beverly Hills, California: Sage Publications, 1987.

Pressman, N. and X. Zepic. *Planning in Cold Climates: A Critical Overview of Canadian Settlement Patterns and Policies.* *Winnipeg, Manitoba:* Institute of Urban Studies, University of Winnipeg (Winter Communities Series No. 1), 1986.

Pressman, N. *Reshaping Winter Cities* (editor). Waterloo, Ontario: University of Waterloo Press & Livable Winter City Association, 1985.

Rapoport, A. "Learning about settlements and energy from historical precedents". *Ekistics.* Vols. 325 (July/August 1987), 326 (September/October 1987), 327 (November/December 1987) Athens, Greece. 1987.

Rautsi, J. "Sustainable Development in Settlement Planning". *Neighbourhood Planning and Housing Design in Cold and Subarctic Areas.* Oslo, Norway: Ministry of Environment, October 1992.

Regional Municipality of Hamilton-Wentworth. *Planning for Low Density: A Solar Approach.* Prepared for the City of Hamilton (Ontario, Canada). July 1980.

Robinette, G.O. (ed.). *Energy Efficient Site Design.* Scarborough, Ontario: Van Nostrand Reinhold, 1983.

Rogers, W. C. "Discovering That Terrible Russian Winter". *Livable Winter Newsletter.* Vol. 4, No. 4. Toronto, Ontario: Livable Winter City Association, August 1986.

Rogers, W.C. and J. Hanson. *The Winter City Book.* Edina, Minnesota: Dorn Books, 1980.

Rowan Williams Davies & Irwin Inc. *Microclimatic Design Guidelines, Windsor Civic Square – Urban Design Study.* Guelph, Ontario (report 91-311T-1), 1991.

Sandrisser, B. "Climate-Responsive Design: Accepting Seasonal Change". *The Yearbook of Landscape Architecture* (The Issue of Energy) – (eds., R. Austin, K. Dawson, T. Mulak, W. Scerbo). New York: Van Nostrand Reinhold, 1985.

Sauzet, M. "A propos du manifeste (de Sanary)". *Le carré bleu: revue international d'architecture,* 2/87. Paris, 1987.

Schoenauer, N. *Design for Energy Conservation in the Sub-Arctic with Special Reference to Fermont.* Seminar on the Impact of Energy Considerations on the Planning and Development of Human Settlements, Economic Commission for Europe, Committee on Housing Building and Planning (special paper). Ottawa, Ontario: October 3-14, 1977.

Smedal, G. "The Philosophy and Practice of Colours". *Neighbourhood Planning and Housing Design in Cold and Subarctic Areas.* Oslo, Norway: Ministry of Environment, October 1992.

Supic, P. "Vernacular Architecture: A Lesson of the Past for the Future". *The Impact of Climate on Planning and Building.* (A. Bitan, ed.). Lausanne, Switzerland: Elsevier Sequoia S.A., 1982.

Swiss National Tourist Office. *Popular Customs and Festivals in Switzerland.* (2nd edition). Zurich, 1990.

Torsson, B. *Places in Town: On Topographical Qualities of Urban Space.* Working Paper delivered at the Swedish-American Architectural Research Seminar. Stockholm: Royal Institute of Technology (KTH). June 14-18, 1982.

van Ginkel, B. Lemco. "New Towns in the North". *Contact: New Communities in Canada* (special issue) – (ed. Norman Pressman). Waterloo, Ontario: University of Waterloo, Faculty of Environmental Studies. 1976.

Verge, R.W. and G.P. Williams. "Drift Control". *Handbook of Snow: Principles, Processes, Management and Use.* D.M. Gray and D.H. Male (eds.). Toronto, Ontario: Pergamon Press, 1981.

Winter Cities Forum – Symposium Proceedings. Edmonton, Alberta (February 15-19). 1986.

Wurtmann, R.J. and J.J. Wurtmann. "Carbohydrates and Depression", *Scientific American*. 260 (1), 1989.

Ylimaula, A-M., R. Niskasaari, and I. Okkonen. *The Oulu School of Architecture: Towards the New Millenium*. Helsinki: The Finnish Building Centre, 1993.

Zrudlo, L. *Psychological Problems and Environmental Design in the North*. Québec, Canada: University of Laval, Collection Nordicana, No. 34., 1972.

Zuckermann, W. *End of the Road*. Post Mills, Vermont: Chelsea Green Publishing Company, 1991.

AUTHOR'S BIOGRAPHICAL DATA

Norman Pressman is Professor of Planning and Urban Design, School of Urban and Regional Planning, University of Waterloo, Ontario, and founding president of the Winter Cities Association. Internationally known, he has published widely in the fields concerned with urban design and 'winter cities' research, and lectures on the subjects of public policy, design, and development planning with emphasis upon cold-climate regions.

He has consulted for United Nations agencies orchestrating international colloquia on human settlement planning in northern regions. Since 1984 he has been invited to speak about this issue in Sweden, Norway, Denmark, Iceland, Finland, Switzerland, Germany, Austria, The Netherlands, Canada, and the U.S.A. At the Winter Cities Forum '90, Tromsø, Norway, he was a member of the team which received an International Winter Cities 'Award of Excellence'. Co-author (with Prof. Jorma Mänty) of the books *Cities Designed for Winter* (1988) and (with Boudewijn Bach) *Climate-Sensitive Urban Space* (1992) he teaches a unique course on winter planning and design at the University of Waterloo.

Most recently, during the 1991 September-December period, Professor Pressman was invited 'Research Fellow' at the Delft University of Technology, Faculty of Architecture, The Netherlands; Fellow at the Salzburg Seminar (1992); and a keynote speaker at the Winter Cities Forum '94 held in Anchorage, Alaska.

Member of the Canadian Institute of Planners, the Ontario Professional Planners Institute, and the American Institute of Certified Planners, he is active in a broad range of circumpolar endeavours.